Children of Poverty

Studies and Dissertations on the Effects of Single Parenthood, the Feminization of Poverty, and Homelessness

Stuart Bruchey
UNIVERSITY OF MAINE

General Editor

A Garland Series

The Deserving Poor

Jeffry A. Will

Garland Publishing, Inc.
New York & London
1993

Library of Congress Cataloging-in-Publication Data

Will, Jeffry A.
    The deserving poor / Jeffry A. Will.
        p.   cm. — (Children of poverty)
    Includes bibliographical references and index.
    ISBN 0-8153-1122-2 (alk. paper)
    1. Public welfare—United States—Public opinion. 2. Welfare recipients—United
States—Public opinion. 3. Poverty—Government policy—United States—Public
opinion. 4. Public opinion—United States. I. Title.
HV95.W54   1993
362.5'0973—dc20
                                                                92–36022
                                                                CIP

Printed on acid-free, 250-year-life paper
Manufactured in the United States of America

In Memory of

JORDAN TRAVIS BROWN

1982-1988

CONTENTS

TABLES

FIGURES

PREFACE

This manuscript represents the fruits of a wonderful, enlightening, yet incomplete journey into the realm of public opinion and inequality. This journey has served more to pose questions than answer them. It has served to wet the desire for further understanding rather than quench the thirst for knowledge. When I first began this project in 1986 I was enlisted to help with the technical details of constructing the primary research instrument examined within these pages. It was only after I became intimately involved with the technical process that I was encouraged by Peter Rossi to tackle the intellectual challenge posed by the task. This was the most important and powerfully positive task I accepted since beginning my professional development.

In 1986, we were just beginning to gain a grasp of the immense problems that were rising out of the recession of the mid 1980's. William J. Wilson had not released his prophetic concern for the truly disadvantaged. Homelessness and the plight of the poor was still a major news item. Reporting the touching scenes of homeless families and children in food lines was the norm for Dan, Ted, and Tom. It appeared that the issue of poverty had regained the center ring previously held in the mid 1960s and during the great depression. The plight of the disadvantaged had become a major concern of the public.

Although this concern still exists for a number of social scientists, its emphasis within the public sphere during the 1990s appears less powerful. This has been felt most often on personal note. In 1990 while finishing the original version of this project, I polled my students at the University of Massachusetts about the "three most pressing social problems in America." Everyone in the class listed homelessness or poverty as the problem most feared: Racism was a close third. In fall 1992, the same question was posed to my students at Virginia Commonwealth University. Only one student in 90 listed homelessness as one of the three most pressing social problems - only a handful listed racial issues. Perhaps the times are a'changin'.

As this manuscript goes to press we are approaching the election of 1992. The United States in is the midst of a major and prolonged recession. The number of Americans falling below the poverty line has reached its highest level since the mid 1960s. Unemployment is higher than during the recession of the mid 1980s. Americans are overextended financially, and are concerned about the level of taxes they pay--all the more important considering we still pay lower overall taxes than citizens in almost any other industrialized nation. George Bush and Bill Clinton are vying to be the one to solve these problems. Both want to reduce spending on social programs. Both believe that the answer to the problems of the poor resides in hard work--although one acknowledges that some assistance may be needed for those who truly need and deserve it.

A lot has happened within the American economic and political arenas since the data presented here were collected in mid 1986. For that reason, some of the conclusions may be somewhat muted. We do believe, however, that the general thrust of the findings remains. The American belief in helping one's neighbor still seems to be intact. The response to the devastation from several natural disasters over recent years helps underscore this belief. Some specifics may be effected, but not the overall conscience.

In this study we examine how the American public views poor families, and the extent to which these families deserve assistance. These findings offer insight into how Americans judge their neighbors, and the level of support they will offer.

I am not normally grouped with optimists. The findings presented here, however, appear to counter the "common" perception that Americans are insensitive to the needs of the less fortunate in our society. This study cannot claim to have determined positively that the American public is made up of only "good Samaritans." It is hoped, however, that it will help open up a discussion as to where we stand.

ACKNOWLEDGMENTS

This manuscript was originally written in February 1990 as part of my doctoral work in Sociology at the University of Massachusetts, Amherst. Although I believe that I have corrected some of the shortcomings of that edition, those persons who have assisted throughout the process deserve special mention here. No intellectual endeavor is truly an "independent" project. In developing our theses we are all enhanced by the input from friends, co-workers, and critics alike. We may ultimately be the solo author of a piece of prose, but we are hardly the sole producer of that product. With that in mind, I would like to make a few remarks for the many people who have been with me throughout this experience, offering (as Doctor Bhavani Sitaraman so accurately quoted our friend Dr. Lam) both "moral and immoral" support.

First, I thank my mentor and, most importantly, my friend Peter Rossi for his support and encouragement while guiding me through the earlier version of this work. Peter took an interest in my work and my well being early on in my tenure as a graduate student. Although time and distance have separated us, and various other reasons have kept us from further work together, he has continued to be a major inspiration for me. His dedication to the discipline of Sociology, his penchant for improving our understanding of the forces facing our work, and his genuine concern for the plight of fellow human beings, attributes frequently overlooked by his critics, serves as a guide for this, and all of my work. He was able to push me, and to offer support to me in ways that only people who know Peter Rossi as well as I can appreciate.

I also thank my friends and colleagues at the University of Massachusetts: To Andy Anderson for his guidance, support, and friendship throughout these years. Words can hardly convey the thanks and debt I owe him. To Mike Lewis for his perseverance in making sure that this product would come to completion--yet not at the cost of burnout or frustration. My friends Doug Anderton and N.

Jay Demerath were particularly helpful in keeping me focused during the "home stretch" that cold Winter of 1990.

Additionally, I thank my colleagues from the West Machmer Marian Society, Dee Weber, Bhavani Sitaraman, Deb Sellers, and Harpo Power. Their support during the finishing phases of this project will forever be appreciated. In addition, I am grateful for the support offered by my colleagues Georgianna Willis, Julie Lam, Steve Lilly and Rhys Williams. I want to thank my friend Anne Balazs, who put up with the disappointments, frustrations, and successes involved in this process in ways that go above and beyond the call.

Also, I thank my former colleagues at the University of Oklahoma. Their support, materially as well as personally and emotionally, carried me through some rough times. A special note of thanks to my friends Bob Bursik, Harold Grasmick, John Cochran, and Mitch Chamlin. Jennifer Bursik deserves special mention for her assistance in cleaning up the manuscript for publication. The Oklahoma experience would not have been complete without the help and support of my students and friends Bruce Arneklev, Kent Bausman, Ashley Cole, Chase Cole, Mark Edwards, and Melanie McCourry, as well as the more than 1500 students whose names I cannot list here.

On a more clearly social level, I thank members of the North Amherst/Leverett Goat Ropers Association, including Robert Bourke, Joe Nowicki, Ed Mann, and Roger Rhinehart for their friendship and support over the past 10 years. Also, I would like to thank the great people from the Eddington Street Coral and The Deli in Norman, OK, for their support during my brief, yet very memorable, stay in Oklahoma. The political debates served as a reminder that "common" folks are hardly common. A note of thanks must also be extended to the James River Rugby Club, Richmond, VA, for allowing me to work out the frustrations of putting together the final touches on this manuscript.

I am very grateful to my new colleagues at the Department of Sociology and Anthropology at Virginia Commonwealth University. Their assistance in the final presentation of this work barely scratches the surface of their dedication to the discipline, and the level of support they have shown me. Most important of all, I want to thank all of my friends and colleagues who I may have missed in the preceding list. The extent of their support is immeasurable.

Finally, I thank Joseph Pereira and Lois Thessien Love for the help and assistance in providing the additional data sets needed for this analysis.

In closing, I acknowledge the love and support I have received from my family throughout my college and graduate school years, and that I still enjoy today. I thank my mother and father, Thelma and Ramon Will, for their love and support during my extended absence from the homestead. Thanks also to my siblings, Larry, Theresa, Michael, Mark, Greg, Brian and Barbara, and their spouses. I would also like to acknowledge my nephews and nieces: Denise, Justin, Devin, Brittany, Ramon, Blake, Christopher, Logan, Lindsey, and all others that are to be born. If not for them, my work in Sociology would be an empty journey.

I have dedicated this book to the memory of my nephew Jordan Travis Brown. I never really got to know Jordan--he was killed in an automobile accident in January, 1988. He was 5 years old. Despite the tragic loss of such a young and beautiful child, his spirit and independence live on in his family and in my life. I can only imagine how his death will ultimately effect members of my family, and how our lives would have been enhanced were he still alive today.

As I suggested at the beginning of these acknowledgments, no endeavor of this magnitude is ever completed by one's self. Although what ultimately wound up in this book is my responsibility, those mentioned above are the ones who carried me through this journey.

Jeffry A. Will
Richmond, VA
September, 1992

The Deserving Poor

CHAPTER 1

WHY STUDY PUBLIC PERCEPTIONS OF WELFARE AND WELFARE RECIPIENTS?

INTRODUCTION.

Debate over welfare reform, funding for social programs and spending priorities has re-emerged in force over the past few years after almost two decades of dormancy from the headlines. The increases in homelessness, particularly among young families, and the drastic increase in the inner-city poor, have forced legislators and the public to re-evaluate the nature of poverty and the role of the welfare system in protecting those who suffer from that poverty. Ronald Reagan's 1986 call for a "re-examination" of the welfare system, George Bush's "kinder, gentler America," juxtaposed with his "read my lips, NO new taxes" campaign, and various welfare reform initiatives floating around congress only serve to underscore the scope of this re-evaluation.

Yet, legislative arguments over spending priorities for social welfare programs often center upon "what the people will tolerate," with regard to taxation for, and coverage of, the existing or proposed programs. For the most part, these arguments are based more on ideological suppositions, with evidence being used for political expediency as much as for analysis. This is not to say that lawmakers are indifferent, or oblivious to what evidence does exist. Rather, the evidence that does exist is used only sparingly, and only in certain circumstances.

This study is about popular perceptions of poverty and welfare entitlements. More specifically, this study is about how to assess information on what "the people will tolerate" with regard to assistance to victims of poverty, and to examine the ways in which

3

such toleration, or "generosity", is affected by the conditions those victims experienced. Three studies, all of which were conducted between 1980 and 1986, will be addressed in order to examine the perceptions of poverty and the extent of generosity toward the poor. In each of these studies, various approaches using the Factorial Survey methodology were used to examine levels of generosity toward the poor.

In this analysis, three primary concerns about the limits of poverty and generosity will be addressed. First, from a methodological point of analysis, we will examine the variations in the application of the Factorial Survey method found in these three studies. Through the examination of these different attempts at measuring generosity, the underlying factors which affect these perceptions of poverty can be compared and contrasted. Differences in perceptions of the needs of those suffering from poverty over the periods covered by these studies, and methodological differences between the studies will be addressed in this section.

Second, from a more substantive point of analysis, a more in depth examination of attitudes about, and conceptions of, the poor and the lower limits of poverty will be conducted using one of these studies, the 1986 General Social Survey, the major annual national probability sample survey conducted in the social sciences. Specifically, what are the boundaries of our social responsibility for the poor? At what point, and for what types of persons, should a minimum income floor be established?

Finally, a comparison of public attitudes and prevailing public policy will serve as a backdrop for a discussion of the social policy implications the findings from these studies offer.

THE STUDIES.

To understand conceptions of poverty, the poor, and what should be done to assist those affected, it is essential to understand the ramifications of the methods that have been employed to assess these conceptions. In the following chapters, an examination of three distinct applications of a relatively new method of inquiry - the Factorial Survey - is used to address the complexities faced when assessing public opinion. These studies include a 1984 study in Chicago by Lois Thiessen Love and Dwight Frankfather, a 1984 study by Joseph Pereira and Peter H. Rossi, and the 1986 General Social

Survey. A brief description of these data sets and methods is needed here.

Love and Frankfather: The Chicago Study.

The Love and Frankfather study (Love, 1986) was conducted in Chicago and the Cook County area in late summer, 1984. Respondents were selected from a random sample of registered voters taken from the Chicago and Cook County voting roles. With a mail questionnaire survey going to one (1) randomly selected voter taken from the voter list for each precinct selected for the study (360 precincts form Chicago, and 288 from the surrounding Cook County area), a total of 258 respondents participated in the Chicago study.

Pereira and Rossi: New York City.

The Pereira and Rossi (Pereira, 1989) study was conducted in New York City in 1984. This originally was designed as a pilot study to explore the potential benefits to be derived from the Factorial Survey. Pereira and Rossi's study was based on a sample of 200 English speaking residents of New York City, ranging in age from 18 to 64. The sample was collected by using a block quota sampling strategy, selecting appropriate blocks so as to insure that a heterogeneous sample was obtained. Interviewers from the National Opinion Research Center were sent to these blocks, and assigned age and gender quotas for the interviews. Research on this study was conducted in February and March, 1984.

The General Social Survey 1986: The National View.

The primary analysis for this monograph will be concerned with a description of attitudes and conceptions of the "deserving and undeserving" poor, by utilizing the 1986 General Social Survey. The General Social Survey (GSS) is a national probability sample survey conducted each year[1] by the National Opinion Research Center at the University of Chicago. In the 1986 survey, both conventional survey items dealing with conceptions of the welfare recipients and social policies directed toward poor people, and a supplemental Factorial Survey section were employed to address respondents' perceptions of what characteristics suggest persons are deserving of welfare assistance.

WHY STUDY PERCEPTIONS?: THE CURRENT STATE OF AFFAIRS.

The primary reason employed here for studying the perceptions of welfare is so that some measure, or barometer, can be developed for use in devising and implementing social policies aimed at alleviating the problems of the poor. In a democratic society the implementation of public policy often relies on the support, and tax revenues, of the members of that society. Obtaining statistics on the conditions of the residents of this country is relatively easy. Ascertaining how much money individuals and families earn, from legal and "over the table" sources at least, is already routinized in the tax and income reporting laws.

Yet what is done with the information gained from this routine is not as straightforward or routinized. Debates over the meaning of the income disparities we see when examining the American public, and what, if anything, should be done to reduce those disparities, are far from resolved. How do we decide what constitutes being poor? Once that is decided, how do we determine need? Once "poor" and "needy" are determined, how much do we give by way of assistance?

In order to devise appropriate programs and policy to deal with the problems of poverty we need to be aware of both the actual conditions of the population under consideration and the perceptions of that population held by those who may not be currently affected by those conditions. For the purposes of this study, the discussion that follows will be concerned primarily with the eligibility requirements and benefit levels of programs affecting non-elderly families and children, primarily the Aid to Families with Dependent Children (AFDC) program.

Poverty Definitions and Levels.

The actual definition of the "poverty line" used to determine of assistance eligibility varies between states, and between states and the Federal Government. The official Federal poverty level in the U.S. in 1986, as defined by the Social Security Administration, was based on the "economy diet" formula developed by Orshansky (1965) for the Department of Agriculture. The poverty threshold represented 3 times the cost of that diet, and thus varied in actual level depending on family composition (Love, p. 3). "The poverty Index is based solely on money income and does not reflect... non-cash benefits such as food stamps, medicaid, and public housing." (*Statistical Abstracts of the United States*, 1989, p. 419)

In 1986, the maximum yearly income for a single person living alone, and still considered below the poverty line was $5,778. The income cutoff for the poverty line for a family of four in that same year, $11,611, represents only slightly more than twice the amount for a single person. Using this definition, more than 32 million Americans, or almost 14 percent of the population fell below the poverty line in 1986. More than 43 million Americans, about 18 percent, fell below 125 percent of the official poverty line in 1986 (*Statistical Abstracts*, 1989).

Meeting the requirements for receipt of some assistance for the 32 million who fall below the poverty line is easier for some than others: assessing AFDC eligibility for a young mother with two children is relatively straightforward; a single, young, male has much more difficulty qualifying for general relief assistance. More importantly, the benefit levels for most programs vary even more widely than the criterion from between states, or the federal government. Although Social Security benefits and eligibility requirements are set primarily by the federal government, public assistance programs for the non-elderly, non-handicapped, segment of the population are set by the individual states.

The State Role: Variations in Regulating the Poor.

To be considered for government assistance in most States, citizens must meet the criteria of a "market value approach," which may include costs for housing, clothing, and transportation, as well as food (Love, p. 3). Using one version of the market value approach, which includes housing and food assistance as income, more than 29 million Americans would still fall below the poverty line (as compared to almost 33 million when the current poverty definition is used).

However, many studies have shown that this results in widely varied standards from state to state (Love, 1986, Shapiro and Greenstein, 1988, Newman and Schnare, 1988). That is, in order to receive welfare or government assistance, an applicant must be found to be in need of assistance according to criteria set by individual states. Meeting the requirements in Illinois, for example, does not necessarily indicate that someone would meet the requirements in Indiana.

Typically, variations in state regulations, eligibility requirement, and benefit levels are drastically different. For example, average 1986 benefit levels for recipients of Aid to Families with Dependent Children (AFDC) in Alabama was approximately $114 per month, while in neighboring Tennessee, AFDC payments averaged $143 per month. In Minnesota, on the other hand, AFDC recipients averaged more than $500 per month in benefits,
while AFDC payments in neighboring South Dakota averaged only about $266 per month (*Statistical Abstracts of the United States*, 1989, p. 367).

Of course, some variation in actual cash payment levels of some assistance programs is understandable. Costs of living vary among different states. Living expenses in New York would be expected to be greater than those in Tennessee. Yet, as can be seen when comparing neighboring states, these differences appear to be less associated with cost of living and more with political factors, for payment levels, even in some of the "best" states, do not serve as enough to truly support poor families, and not all programs are available to all persons in all states. These variations in state levels of support and in program availability have an impact upon the ability for recipients to take control of their lives and get out of the poverty ranks.

In their detailed analysis of the variations in public assistance levels and coverage, Shapiro and Greenstein (1988) found that only one out of nine families with young children who otherwise would have been poor were lifted out of poverty by the cash assistance they received. Indeed, their analysis shows that, with the exception of Alaska, the cash assistance from combined benefits received from AFDC and the dollar value from food stamps is not enough to pull a family of three from any state out of poverty without additional income (Shapiro and Greenstein, p.54). In only six states does income from these assistance programs lift such families above 90 percent of the poverty line. Similarly, they show that only in 19 states does the assistance level total 50 percent or more of the poverty level for a family of three (Shapiro and Greenstein, p.39).

Coverage of those persons who fall below the poverty line eligible for assistance also varies widely between various states and programs. Eligibility requirements for public assistance programs differ between states for both intact families and single individuals single. Shapiro and Greenstein show that in 23 states, two-parent families do not receive AFDC benefits. In addition, pregnant women and children are eligible for Medicaid assistance in only one half of the states. In only eight states are general assistance (GA) payments not restricted to elderly and handicapped individuals (Shapiro and Greenstein, p.39).

The Federal Role: The Need for Continuity.

If, as Shapiro and Greenstein suggest, the disparities between states and program support represents more than merely cost of living differences, a strong argument could then be made for a uniform, federally designed and enforced set of eligibility requirements and benefit levels. Constitutional protections supersede states' rights on a variety of other areas of public life, particularly areas concerning legislative representation, equal protection under the law and basic due process rights. If, as Shapiro and Greenstein, and others, argue that citizens of various states are not equally protected under the public assistance program criteria, then perhaps federal attention should be focused on the creation of standards that would ensure all persons such protections.

A portion of the disparities within levels of support between states can be traced to economically depressed regions. However, that not all of the disparity can be explained in this manner suggests the need for federal efforts at standardization. Even for those regions in which support levels do closely resemble the economic decline of the region, Federal standards could prove to be quite beneficial. Indeed, as Rossi (1989) suggests, the effects of such Federal guidelines could actually serve to reduce the long term costs of standardization of welfare programs by improving the health of those on welfare and re-establishing that portion of the population in the private economy.

PUBLIC OPINION AND PUBLIC POLICY.

The brief discussion of the variations in state run public assistance programs presented here, and the subsequent discussion of the need for implementing federal guidelines for these programs is only part of the answer for beneficial welfare reform. As we can see in the previous discussion, measuring the extent to which poverty exists is relatively simple. The data available in this country cover a wide variety of aspects of the economic life in the United States. In addition, we can easily examine disparities between the states and regions of this country with regard to how the government deals with the "economic reality" facing the poor. An important, and primarily unexamined, area of concern with regard to dealing with issues of welfare and public assistance is public opinion and perceptions of what the government can, and should, do to alleviate poverty.

Arguments over the role of public opinion in developing public policy are not easy to develop or defend. On the one hand, the challenge of democracy is to involve the public in the legislative process, and thus it is important to understand and include the wants and opinions of the public when devising public policy. On the other hand, democracy also demands that the "tyranny of the masses" be avoided when actually implementing that policy.

The fact is, public opinion about the issues at hand IS used by state and federal law makers when policy is developed. Law makers consistently cite public opinion and the "desires of their constituency" - their "boss" - when voting on social programs. Thus it is important to study those opinions in order to understand what the constituents' needs and wants are, although not necessarily for precise decisions on action.

The primary purpose of this study, therefore, is to show that, like actual poverty rates and program payments, opinion can be measured, and that those measures of opinion should be used in policy discussion. Most importantly, however, since these opinions are used as arguments for social policy, these opinions must be measured well.

THE PLAN.

Public perceptions of the needs of the poor, and perceptions of whose responsibility it is to provide public assistance, are essential ingredients for effective program development. In the following chapters, we will look at what those perceptions are, how they can be measured, and how they can affect policy development.

In Chapter 2, we will examine a variety of research that has addressed perceptions of the poor. Over the past two decades, a number of studies have addressed attitudes toward the poor and welfare programs. These include both quantitative attitudinal items used in surveys, as well as theoretical statements on the underlying issues surrounding public assistance and program development.

In Chapter 3, we will examine how the three studies discussed above attempted to assess the underlying mechanisms of how perceptions of the poor are based. In particular, we will compare how the design of each of these studies serves to improve our understanding of public perceptions.

Finally, Chapters 4 and 5 provide a detailed analysis of the 1986 General Social Survey vignette component. As the only available study that examines perceptions of the poor in depth with a nationally representative sample, analysis of the GSS will allow for a better understanding of the public's levels of generosity toward the economically disadvantaged segment of the population.

NOTES

1. The GSS actually has been conducted each year since 1972, with the exception of 1979 and 1981. It has been based on a National Probability Sample since 1975. For most years, supplemental sections of the survey are added in order to focus on particular methodological or substantive issues.

CHAPTER 2

PREVIOUS EXAMINATIONS OF ATTITUDES TOWARD WELFARE ISSUES: A REVIEW OF RELEVANT LITERATURE

INTRODUCTION

Public opinion surveys on social welfare programs are hardly a new phenomenon. Indeed, systematic polling of public attitudes toward social service programs has been chronicled from as early as the Great Depression Years and the New Deal legislation (Shiltz, 1970). Of primary importance in these studies, however, were poverty and income issues facing the elderly and issues involved in the creation of Social Security and Medicaid programs.[1] Only a few studies have been primarily devoted to analyzing public opinion with regard to support for the non-elderly poor in this country. Instead, most analysis of public opinion on non-elderly welfare related issues has come from single items or a short battery of items included in general interest surveys.

The results of those inquiries that have been undertaken to assess the public's perceptions and acceptance of social welfare have been strangely mixed. On the one hand, we find the public is strongly in favor of support for the elderly and the "assistance to the poor." On the other hand, however, we find little support for wealth redistribution policies and a distaste on the part of the public for "welfare" (Smith, 1987). In addition, while the overall levels of **public** support for social programs to help the elderly and the poor have remained stable over the past decades, (Shapiro et al., 1987a) legislative support has been less stable and debate more rancorous (Cook, et. al., 1988).

This chapter reviews past research that examines three primary areas of interest concerning welfare and public assistance for the non-elderly poor. First, we will examine a variety of items addressing the public's perceptions of "who" is responsible for assisting the poor. Second, a variety of questions have been included in past surveys which assess respondents' perceptions of public assistance spending levels and priorities. Finally, we will examine a number of items that look at perceptions of welfare recipients in general.

REDISTRIBUTION, EQUALITY AND RESPONSIBILITY.

In her discussion of why there is no successful socialist party in the United States - and whether that reason arises from a lack of interest from those who would most benefit from such a system - Hochschild (1981) states that between 1937 and the 1976, only eight questions were included in national surveys addressing issues of redistribution.[2] Half of those items were asked between 1937 and 1939, the middle of the Depression years. For those items, only one-third or less of the respondents agreed with items supporting heavy taxation of the rich. Only 15 percent of respondents on another survey in 1939 supported confiscation of excessive wealth for re-distributive purposes. A 1976 survey item presented by Hochschild, however, found that 47 percent of the respondents agreed that "the government should tax the rich heavily in order to redistribute wealth." (Hochschild, p. 118).

When examining items presented by Hochschild about limiting the total income individuals could earn, a 1939 survey found only 24 percent of the overall population supported such moves, with only 32 percent of the poorest respondents agreeing. Similar items in 1969 and 1976 found increasingly fewer adults supporting income limits, with the percent agreeing only reaching 13 percent overall in 1969 (14 percent of the poorest respondents), to 9 percent in 1976 (the same figure for the poorest respondents).

In analyzing those items, Hochschild states that these questions, as well as other available survey information, show that "more poor than rich support progressive taxation and anti-poverty measures, but seldom do a majority do so." She concludes that "These data give us no clear general picture of support for redistribution - never mind consistent and intelligible details" (Hochschild, 1981 p. 16).

Similarly "inconsistent" results are found when examining two 1976 Harris Poll items. In these surveys, the largest portion of respondents opposed "using the federal government to make a fairer distribution of wealth in this country," although by only a small percent (Shapiro et al., 1987a. p. 127). Indeed, even during the late 1960s, the height of the most recent government effort to establish a guaranteed annual income, surveys also showed a strong public opposition to minimum guaranteed incomes even if that income was less than the poverty line (Ibid).

Yet, despite the lack of evidence supporting guaranteed incomes or forced redistribution of income and resources, Hochschild and others have found that large percentages of the American public do believe that the government has the responsibility for dealing with and ameliorating poverty, with significant levels of support for carrying out such responsibility even if it requires increased taxation (Shiltz, 1970 p. 153; Cook, et al., 1988 p. i). A variety of surveys over the past 40 years have included items that address the extent to which the public believes the government has responsibility, at least in part, for helping the unemployed - or providing employment, providing medical and other assistance to the poor and for eliminating various other problems faced by the poor.

Unemployment and Providing Jobs.
Throughout the past 40 years, a number of items have been included in surveys addressing the government's role in providing for employment and, in the case of those without work, unemployment benefits. Through the examination of many of these items, however, it appears that typically these items address more than merely employment concerns, and include general welfare issues as underlying components of the questions being addressed. Indeed, Shapiro, et al. (1987b), in their review of survey items assessing "Employment and Social Welfare," the items discussed deal directly (or in the case of child care concerns, indirectly) with providing employment for those who want it, and assistance for those who do not work.

Thus "Social Welfare" is inextricably tied to employment concerns. This is not to say that such "ties" are inappropriate, but rather to acknowledge that a strong measure of public support for welfare in general can be seen in support measures for employment concerns specifically. By examining the perceptions of the responsibility of the government to help the unemployed, a more general understanding of government responsibility to the poor emerges.

In a number of surveys conducted throughout the depression and into World War II, Shiltz (1970) found that large proportions of the population believed the government was responsible for helping the unemployed. Shiltz shows that for the survey items of that time, the proportion of the population that believed the government was responsible for helping provide employment to those who needed work rose from 61 percent in 1939 to a high of 79 percent in 1945. Similar items between 1939 and 1945 fluctuated to around 70 percent of the respondents believing the government had responsibility for providing employment. Shiltz also notes that such support waned after the "watershed years during the war," to a low of 45 percent support for government providing employment in 1947, and stabilized with support for such employment staying in the upper 50 percent range through 1960 (Shiltz, 1970, p. 98).

Similar items addressing the government's responsibility for helping the unemployed showed public support levels of more than 60 percent throughout the late depression and World War II period. Although Shiltz concludes that "no clear trend is apparent" from these results, a minimum "floor" of support can be seen wherein two-thirds of the population at that time felt the government had a responsibility to help the unemployed. (Ibid)

In surveys conducted in later years, the proportion of the population supporting the belief that the government has responsibility for providing jobs to those who want them increased dramatically, returning to levels present during the World War II years. Confirming Shiltz's reporting of results from the late 1950's, in a set of items from the National Election surveys of 1956 through 1960 Shapiro et al. (1987a, 1987b) report that from 56 percent (1956) to 58 percent (1960) of the population believed that "the government in Washington should see to it that everyone who wants to work can find a job." Surveys conducted by the CBS television network indicate that proportion increased to as high as 73 percent in May of that 1976, and up to 74 percent in 1978 (Shapiro et al., 1987b, p.274). Almost unanimous support was found in two consecutive 1972 Harris Polls, with 87 percent and 89 percent of those persons interviewed favoring "a federal program to give productive jobs to the unemployed" (Ibid, p. 276).

Similarly high levels of support for government action with regard to expanding employment were found in a series of surveys conducted by Trendex, Inc. between 1966 and 1982. In these surveys, respondents were asked whether they would like the "government to do more, do less, or do about the same as they have been on...expanding employment." In all, this item was included in more than 45 surveys between 1966 and 1982. In only four of these surveys (February, 1966, January 1968, February 1969 and February 1980) did less than 60 percent of the respondents respond that the government should do more, with the lowest percent suggesting an increase in government effort of 56 percent in January of 1968. For most of the surveys, public support for an increase in government effort remained stable at around 65 percent (plus or minus 3 percent).

Note, however, that some items discussed by Shapiro, et. al. show a less distinct pattern of support for government responsibility for employment. In a series of items used in The National Election surveys and those conducted by Market Opinion Research throughout the 1970s, questions concerning the government's responsibility for maintaining employment/ unemployment benefits were combined with standard of living concerns; thus respondents were asked to respond to a scale wherein one extreme indicated the respondents belief that the government should "see to it that every person has a job and a good standard of living," and the other extreme stated that the government should "let each person get ahead on his own..." For these items, researchers found little with regard to a distinct pattern except a slight tendency for respondent answers to be bunched at both ends, and in the "neutral," or middle range of 4 and 5 (on a 7 point scale). As Shapiro concludes about these items, "...there is apparently substantial variation in response depending on how questions are phrased..." (Shapiro, et al., 1987b, p. 269).

Responsibility for Health and Welfare.
According to Shiltz (1970), the measuring of public support for the government providing health care for poor persons, elderly and young, has been complicated in the past by the divisive debate in the legislature over Medicare, Medicaid and various "national health insurance" proposals put before Congress. In addition, Shiltz cites problems in interpreting opinion poll results from the 1930s through the 1960s because of the lack of an actual program about which respondents could respond, and the tendency for such polls to actually introduce non-informed citizens to various program propos-

als. Indeed, the lack of a public informed about various health care proposals, and the intense opposition to such programs waged by the American Medical Association, often resulted in vastly different support levels for even similar program proposals or differently worded items addressing the same programs (Shiltz, 1970 p. 129-131).

Despite this variation among specific program support, however, Shiltz argues that:

> "Running through this 30-year period of legislative skirmishes was a consistent pattern of strong public support for the principle of government action to alleviate the high costs of medical care. This support pattern was modified by a substantial cleavage across class levels and by a small, but increasing, tendency for older Americans to support the principle more often than younger citizens." (p. 128)

Shiltz cites seven national studies conducted between 1936 and 1964 in which respondents were asked whether they agreed that "government ought to help people get doctors' and hospital care at low cost." In each of these surveys except the last, more than 60 percent of the respondents agreed (at least with a qualified positive response) that low-cost health care was a government responsibility. Surveys taken from 1936 to 1942 show that three quarters of the population believed health care was the government's responsibility, while only one fifth of the population disagreed. The proportion agreeing dropped to 62 percent in favor and 26 percent opposing government responsibility in 1956, but rebounded to 71 percent supporting government responsibility in health care matters in 1960. In 1964, the proportion supporting government responsibility dipped to 56 percent (although the percent increased to 64 percent when no opinion and non-responses were omitted) - a drop primarily attributed by Shiltz to a change in question wording (p. 128).

More recent survey items that address government responsibility and effort for health care issues report similar public opinion trends. Shapiro, et al., report that in a series of items used in surveys by TRENDEX between 1965 and 1982, when asked about the level of government effort on "Health Measures," a vast majority of respondents in all of the surveys indicated that the government should either "do more" with regard to health measures or at least maintain current levels of effort. In all, more than 49 of these items were used in TRENDEX surveys during this period, and with the exception of 1966 (when 59 percent suggested the government "do more" and 23 percent wanted the level of effort to remain the same), the percent favoring **increased** government activity never fell below 60 percent.

Indeed, throughout the 1970s the proportion of respondents who wanted increased activity on the part of government never fell below 67 percent (the January 1979 level), with support levels of more than 80 percent for all of the surveys conducted in 1972 and as high as 84 and 82 percent in July 1973 and July 1984, respectively. In addition, the percentage of respondents favoring less involvement stayed lower than 15 percent in any of the years in which the item was included. Subsequent items posed to in surveys from 1972 to 1982 also revealed that two thirds of those favoring increased government activity maintained such support even if it would include an increase in taxes (Shapiro, et al., 1986, p. 422).

Program Preference and Spending Levels.
As we have seen from the above discussion, support for government responsibility for maintaining programs to help the poor, unemployed, and infirm in this country appears to be strong, and has remained so over the past 50-60 years. Although such support is not unanimous, significant majorities portions of the population support government involvement. However, we need to also examine the extent to which this support for responsibility is mirrored by support for actual government EXPENDITURES. Government spends money on a variety of public programs, only a portion of which are directed at the poor. Although only a limited number of items examining socialist or re-distributive positions have been included in surveys, more common place are items assessing respondents perceptions of various social welfare programs, and spending priorities for these endeavors.

Indeed, Shiltz (1970) examines a wide variety of survey items assessing respondent preferences for various welfare programs between 1935 and 1965, including social security, national health insurance, unemployment compensation and government work programs, among others. In addition, spending priority items are now mainstays in the most well-known national survey, the annual General Social Survey.

In a review of 15 survey items that assess public support for expenditures for welfare, Shiltz shows a "clear majority" of the population supported either increased spending or at least maintaining the current levels. Indeed, support for **decreasing** welfare expenditures in these 15 surveys was highest in the late depression years (around 39 percent) and decreased to a maximum of 23 percent in favor of spending reductions in the post war years. In addition, Shiltz states that to complement the relatively high levels of spending support, little change was seen in the demographic and social composition of the supporters (p. 152).

Later studies, however, show less consistent support for welfare spending, and often contradictory responses to specific spending items. Indeed, in a review of items between 1971 and the 1986, Shapiro et. al. (1987b) found that when respondents were asked about the levels of government spending for *welfare* specifically, significant proportions of respondents - with levels higher than 50 percent for surveys conducted in 1971, 1973 and between 1976 and 1981 - believed too MUCH was being spent, while only one-fifth of the respondents believed too little was being spent. For each of these surveys, the single largest response category was found for the "too much spending" option. These results were found for 24 different surveys[3] conducted between 1971 and 1986.

We must exercise caution, however, when interpreting the "public sentiment" found in these items. As Smith, 1987, concluded, and as we saw earlier with regard to items assessing government responsibility for employment, question phrasing appears to affect the responses to these items. In his 1987 article examining the affect of question wording on perceptions of welfare spending, Smith compared sets of "experimental" items from various surveys - one type assessing spending priorities for "welfare" and the other assessing spending on "assistance to the poor." In this study, Smith found that agreement for items assessing support for "assistance to the poor" or similar statements averaged more than 39 percentage points higher than items asking about "welfare." Indeed, "welfare consistently produces much more negative evaluations than 'the poor.'" (Smith, 1987 p.76).

Support for increased spending on health care, however, is less ambiguous, and more strongly felt, than the support levels we found for general "welfare" spending. Indeed, in 23 surveys conducted by two different research organizations (Roper and NORC-GSS) between 1971 and 1985, more than 90 percent of all respondents believed that either too little was being spent, or that spending levels were about right for "improving and protecting the nation's health." In none of these surveys did the proportion of those indicating that "**too much** was being spent" exceed 8 percent. For the NORC-GSS studies, support for increasing spending was strongest in the early 1970s, with more than 60 percent feeling too little was being spent through 1976, and leveling off at about 57 percent through the mid 1980s. The proportion of Roper respondents who felt too little was being spent on health issues fluctuated slightly through the late 1970s, reaching a high of 60 percent in 1974 and 1978 surveys. The proportion who felt too little was being spent leveled off at 56 percent through 1983.

WELFARE RECIPIENTS: WHO'S DESERVING?

What often appears to be at the center of the discussion of the effect of item wording on perceptions of government responsibility and/or differences in support for welfare program spending is a concern with respondent perceptions of the welfare recipients. Indeed, Shiltz argues that despite the strong support seen for welfare programs, "the public has at the same time displayed a consistent willingness to impugn dishonesty to welfare recipients" (p. 155).

Public suspicion about the honesty and integrity of welfare recipients has been observed throughout the "history" of welfare program implementation. In one 1964 survey, taken at the start of the "War on Poverty," 67 percent of respondents responded that they believed some or most of recipients are "on relief for dishonest reasons". (Shiltz, 1970). Similar survey items showed that between the 1930s and late 1960s, increasing numbers of respondents believed that persons on relief "could find work if they tried." (Shiltz. 1970, p. 156)

Similar findings, as well as contradictions, can be seen in a 1976 and 1977 survey conducted by Harris Associates. In these surveys, respondents were asked a series of questions addressing respondent perceptions of welfare recipients. When asked to respond to the statement that "it's not right to let people who need welfare to go hungry," 94 percent of those responding agreed; when asked to respond to the statement that "too many women whose husbands have left them with several children have no choice but to go on welfare," three-quarters of the respondents agreed. However, these same respondents also overwhelmingly believed that "too many people on welfare could be working" (89 percent for 1976 and 92 percent for 1977), and vast majorities in both years (86 percent and 89 percent respectively) believed that "too many people on welfare cheat..." Similarly, 51 percent of respondents to a New York Times/CBS poll in 1980, and 40 percent in a re-run of that survey in 1986, believed that "most people who receive money from welfare could get along without it if they tried." (Shapiro, et al., 1987a. p. 124)

Cook, et al. (1988), however, found much less belief that welfare recipients cheated, at least with regard to the most well know programs. When asked whether they believed AFDC recipients were cheating the program, less than 4 percent of the respondents believed "almost all" cheated, and only slightly more than 30 percent believed "more than half" or "almost all" cheated. One-third of the respondents indicated that they believed only a few AFDC recipients cheated. When asked about Medicaid, only 16 percent believed half or most recipients cheated, while more than 45 percent believed that only a few cheated. An interesting comparison can be found when comparing these two items to respondents' beliefs about cheating by Social Security recipients. For this item, Cook, et al., report that less than 1 percent (.8 percent) of the respondents believed that "almost all" social security recipients cheated, with more than 60 percent responding that "only a few" were dishonest.

Problems and Inconsistencies in Welfare Attitude Items.

Two primary implications about the public's attitudes toward welfare, and how those attitudes are measured, can be seen in the preceding discussion. First, it appears that for the most part, majorities, or at least strong minorities, of the public have supported various welfare programs during the past 50 years. Second, however, the method with which these items have been measured and the inconsistencies in the level of support and the programs supported do not allow us to make broad-ranging conclusions or recommendations as to what to do with these findings.

Three primary concerns about these items need to be addressed in this regard. First, as we pointed out at the beginning of the discussion, very little has been done on a national scope to examine the public's perceptions of welfare programs and recipients. Indeed, most of the items discussed above are single items, or items from short batteries of items, appended to national surveys taken over the past 50 or more years. On a national scale, nothing prior to 1986 systematically examines the issues of welfare entitlements, spending priorities or beliefs about welfare recipients.

Two studies, Kluegel and Smith (1986) and Cook, et al. (1988), as well as the 1986 GSS supplement (analyzed here) represent the most comprehensive national studies available released over the past decade. Of course some local studies have been undertaken. The most notable, for our purposes here, are Pereira's 1984 study of New Yorker residents' attitudes toward welfare (conducted with Rossi, and also discussed in the following chapters) and Fay Cook's 1976 study of Chicago. However, considering the impact of welfare on legislative debate, it would seem that a much more extensive body of research would have been undertaken.

The second concern this study attempts to deal with is that of the inconsistency in the responses found in these items. Specifically, the items discussed above suffered from one primary inconsistency - minor wording changes in items drastically affected the levels of support shown toward welfare and welfare recipients. Indeed, as Smith (1987) showed, changing the wording from "welfare" to "assistance to the poor" completely reversed the proportion of those who believed to much (or too little) money was being spent.

Finally, as evident in the concern with the item wording, a problem also exists in that respondents are presented with global questions that ask about issues and policies about which they may have no information. Without information on the program in question, or, for example, the circumstances facing the unemployed persons, these items are considered only "stereotypical" representations, which may or may not represent real situations. Concern with this problem was specifically noted by Shiltz (1970) when he discussed items addressing attitudes toward National Health Care measures and found respondents who knew nothing about the program still held specific opinions about those programs.

A BIT ABOUT METHOD: THE FACTORIAL SURVEY APPROACH

Throughout the discussion of previous studies that look at public attitudes toward welfare, a constant underlying theme appears. Specifically, direct comparisons of these items and the attitudes they attempt to tap are compromised by variations in item wording, situational differences in the year or era they are asked, and, particularly with the items on "welfare," the differential reaction to various question wordings and "buzzwords." Although concerns with the year in which items are asked is somewhat beyond the considerations of this study - indeed, changes over the years is precisely what some of the studies discussed above examined - concerns with the situation under discussion, and item design and wording issues represent an important area of interest for all methodology discussion.

In our everyday conversations with colleagues and friends, arguments are seldom made without being used in some context or another. If, for example, a colleague asks us whether we will support a particular political candidate, we often respond with a noncommittal "it depends." Our choice usually depends on the circumstances surrounding the choice to be made: whether the candidate has a decent track record, or, perhaps, even if that candidate has a realistic chance of winning. Similarly, when we ask colleagues whether they support more controversial issues - for instance capital punishment - responses are often couched in caveats - "it depends on how brutal the crime," or "it depends on whether the crime was premeditated." Even the staunchest supporters of such issues invoke "it depends" when pressed with potentially counter-intuitive and counter-productive measures that support their position (e.g. The propriety of capital punishment for murder when the crime is committed by a minor or mentally retarded individual).

It is precisely this concern with the situation - what the formulation of attitudes toward welfare entitlements and the poor "depend" upon - that lead this analysis toward the Factorial Survey approach. Throughout the following chapters, the primary analysis will focus on the results of several attempts to use the Factorial Survey methodology to get beyond the static, and often ambiguous nature of conventional survey items such as those discussed above, and to examine the situational factors that increase or decrease generosity toward the poor.

The Factorial Survey Design.

The Factorial Survey method was employed in these studies to address these ambiguities of conventional survey items. The Factorial

Survey was developed for the social sciences by Peter H. Rossi in the early 1970s. The Factorial Survey approach has been used in numerous studies to assess the judgement process on issues ranging from conceptions of mental illness (Thurman, Lam, and Rossi, 1986) to definitions of sexual harassment (Rossi and Weber-Burdin, 1983), issues of crime deterrence (Anderson, Harris, and Miller, 1983), attitudes toward abortion (Sitaraman, 1990), and the propriety and desirability of various social interactions (Rossi and Will, 1985).[4]

The Factorial Survey approach is "a melding of randomized experiments and sample surveys applied to the general problem of uncovering the underlying regularity of judgments of complex social objects (Rossi and Will, p. 1)." These "complex social objects," or "vignettes", are short descriptions of situations that are constructed from lists of various personal attributes and behaviors. In the case of this study, these lists represent various characteristics of "typical" welfare families. These attributes and behaviors are randomly selected from lists and are arranged into individual scenarios.

Each vignette consists of broadly defined attributes, called dimensions, that cover such characteristics, as in the case of attitudes toward welfare recipients, number of children, marital status, work status of vignette characters, and current income. Each dimension is composed of various of categories or "levels." Thus a typical level for the dimension "number of children" would be "this family has two children." Levels within each dimension are randomly selected and combined with selected levels from other dimensions. By randomly combining these dimensions and levels, we are able to maintain orthoganality, or independence, among the components, and thus analyze the unique importance of each characteristic.

Once these characteristics are combined to form a short story, respondents are asked to evaluate the level of money these families need on which to get by. The rating scale then is added to each of the vignettes to measure the respondents' understanding of this need. In the case of the studies discussed in the next chapters, these scales were used by the respondents to indicate the level of income assistance the vignette families needed.

The Factorial Survey approach combines the variety of items found in the conventional survey, with the some of the experimental control offered by laboratory research. The inclusion of a variety of dimensions and levels allows us to examine differences in how respondents view various characteristics of, for example, welfare families. Yet the Factorial Survey design also allows for the control of the presentation of those characteristics in experimental fashion, thus allowing us to examine underlying trends and influences in the decision making process. Thus, the Factorial Survey approach offers several distinct advantages to the contemporary survey item design.

First, as we found in the previous review of survey items, there has been some concern about the variations in responses toward responsibility and spending resulting from question wording (cf. Shiltz 1970; Shapiro, et al., 1986 and 1987a,1987b; Smith,1987). Although these authors did acknowledge the problems with item wording, there was little they could do to systematically check the effect of those changes. The Factorial Survey technique, however, allows for exactly that type of examination of slight variations in scenario wording. That is, with the Factorial Survey studies discussed here, we can examine the extent to which, for example, explicitly stating the number of children affects generosity toward the vignette families, or how NOT stating some characteristic can change the perceptions of need.

Similarly, we are able to examine the impact of certain characteristics included in a scenario, while controlling for extraneous, or even counter-active, ones. For example, in the studies discussed above we will see that the number of children in a poor household affects the levels of generosity shown toward that family: the more children, the higher the generosity. Yet we also find that other characteristics, particularly work history and disabilities, also play important roles in determining generosity. With traditional style surveys, to accurately assess the independent impact of all three of these items you would have to include an extensive battery of items, each addressing slight changes in how these characteristics impact on generosity. By design, however, the Factorial Survey allows us to carry out this combination of characteristics and assess these independent effects without inundating respondents with dozens of "yes-no" or "agree-disagree" items.

Finally, the Factorial Survey design allows for a more systematic understanding of complex social situations (i.e. the vignettes) without having to oversimplify the constructed situation. That is, with the Factorial Survey, we can examine decision making processes about, for example, welfare program support, without having to resort to simplistic items or to omit potentially important, yet untested, characteristics. For example, in the previous review of survey items, a number of surveys asked about the government's responsibility to help the unemployed. One problem with these items, it could be argued, is that with these items it is difficult, and often impossible, to estimate how such support for increased spending would be affected if the respondents were told of the current efforts of the unemployed to help themselves by actively looking for work. As we will see in the next chapters, the presence of such an effort on the part of vignette characters has a strong affect on the level of assistance which is awarded.

The point here is not to imply that nothing good comes from standard survey research designs, nor to claim that there are no problems with the Factorial Survey approach. It is important to recognize, however, that the recognized limitations and contradictions of standard item design discussed by Shiltz and others can be best addressed and identified through implementation of comparative and advanced methods. The most promising technique for this process, I believe, is found in the Factorial Survey approach.

In the next chapter, the analysis will focus on comparing three different attempts at using the Factorial Survey technique to examine perceptions of welfare and welfare recipients. In Chapters 4 and 5, the focus will be on one of these attempts, the 1986 GSS, and the variations in how sub-groups of the population are similar or differ in how they structure their decisions concerning generosity.

NOTES

1. This is particularly true with regard to Shiltz's monograph (1970), which is an in-depth examination of the Social Security issues from the depression through 1970. In his report, Shiltz concentrates on the public's perceptions and acceptance of a variety of Social Security based issues, and only returns to non-elderly public assistance programs for comparative purposes. For our purposes here, the discussion will focus on works that look at public opinion on issues facing the non-elderly poor population. For additional studies on attitudes toward public assistance programs for the elderly, see Cook, et al, 1988, and Bonnet-Brunnich, 1984, among others.

2. Although the criteria used by Hochschild in deciding that these eight items are all that existed during this period are not completely known, we have evidence that suggests she was merely unable to find all such items that were available. Indeed, as we will see in the coming discussion, a number of additional national survey items can be found that address the issues of redistribution and responsibility in similar fashion to the ones Hochschild discusses. The purpose of including her designation here is to dramatize the fact that even though more than eight items have been included in national surveys over the years, the number of such items is quite small when compared to the political nature and impact of welfare on our society.

3. These surveys are in fact phases of on-going surveys, the Annual GSS and Roper series. Note, however, that they do represent distinct samples and surveys. The question wording is identical. Questions asked "are we spending too much, too little, or about the right amount on Welfare," and were included in a battery of items addressing government spending on various programs.

4. For a more thorough discussion of the Factorial Survey technique, see *Measuring Social Judgments: The Factorial Survey Approach*, Peter H. Rossi and Steven L. Nock, eds., Sage publications, 1982.

CHAPTER 3

MEASURING GENEROSITY TOWARD THE POOR: A COMPARISON OF THREE STUDIES

INTRODUCTION.

Popular conceptions of who are the poor, and, more importantly for the topics under discussion here, to what extent and under what circumstances do the poor deserve assistance, are not adequately understood by social researchers and policy makers. Various surveys have shown contradictory results, both in comparison to other surveys and within individual surveys. In addition, selective presentation of results from such surveys allows both advocates of increased social spending and opponents of such spending to "prove" their relative positions.

This chapter is about the manner in which perceptions of the poor are measured. Specifically, in the next chapters we will examine two primary methods used in measuring these perceptions--the Factorial survey and the more traditional attitude scale items--as used in three separate studies. These studies include the Chicago study by Lois Thessien Love with Dwight Frankfather, The New York Welfare study by Joseph Pereira and Peter H. Rossi and the 1986 General Social Survey. Before continuing with the examination of the results, a brief discussion of the study designs is necessary.

WELFARE IN CHICAGO: LOVE AND FRANKFATHER

The Love and Frankfather study (hereafter referred to as the "Chicago Study") consisted of a survey of Cook County Illinois, which includes all of the city of Chicago and some Chicago suburbs.[1] The data were collected between late August and November, 1984. In all, 258 respondents participated in the survey.

The Chicago Study employed a limited factorial design using vignettes in the study constructed according to conditions of actual AFDC recipients. These descriptions were derived from interviews with 176 welfare families conducted by Frankfather (1983)[2]. Each respondent received four vignettes, with the first vignette for each respondent being identical. Each vignette consisted of 5 dimensions. Panel A of Table 3.1 presents the dimensions and levels used in the Chicago study vignettes.

Instead of using the full factorial approach as described in Rossi and Anderson (1982) the Chicago study employed an "incomplete within blocks" design in which the researchers divided the 108 vignettes into 36 groups of three vignettes each. These groups, or questionnaires, were then randomly assigned to respondents selected in the sample. Each respondent also received an identical vignette, so that "having the first vignette the same for all respondents allows comparisons of respondents who are given different versions of the questionnaire."

As evident in Panel A of table 3.1, each level is actually a paragraph describing a situation for that dimension. It is important to keep in mind several important ingredients of these vignettes. First, in each vignette, the characters depicted are always women (marital status unstated) with two children aged 3 and 6. Second, each level contains several pieces of information. Thus, for example, the "low" level of Nutrition quality mentions several characteristics of low quality nutrition: a) not being able to provide three meals a day; b) the mother not eating so the children can, poorly balanced diet concerns, and the lack of regular servings of the major food groups. The levels within the other dimensions are similarly complex, covering several aspects of the dimension in each level. In all, a total of 108 vignettes are possible when combining the 5 dimensions and levels.

**TABLE 3.1: Panel A: The Chicago Study
Vignette Dimensions and Levels**

Dimension 1: Nutrition Quality

Level 1: (Low) In her efforts to make ends meet (vig name) finds she cannot provide three meals a day. Frequently she goes without food so her children can eat. The family rarely eats a balanced diet. The children only occasionally have milk, meat, or fruit.

Level 2: (Medium) In her efforts to make ends meet (vig name) finds she can almost always provide three meals a day, although he may be forced to skip meals at the end of the month. Sometimes the family isn't able to have milk, meat, or fruit.

Level 3: (High) In her efforts to make ends meet, (vig name) finds that she can always provide three meals a day and enough for everyone. The children always have milk, but occasionally don't eat meat.

Dimension 2: Neighborhood Quality

Level 1: (Low) (Name) and her two children, ages 3 and 6, live in a neighborhood with abandoned buildings and trash on the street. It isn't a very safe neighborhood, day or night. The police take a long time when called.

Level 2: (Medium)(Name) and her two children, ages 3 and 6, live in a neighborhood where the roads need constant repair, but there isn't much litter on the street. It's not the safest neighborhood, but the police come quickly when called.

Level 3: (High) (Name) and her two children, ages 3 and 6, live in an attractive neighborhod that is very safe. The police protection is excellent.

TABLE 3.1: Panel A: The Chicago Study (continued)
Vignette Dimensions and Levels

Dimension 3: Housing Condition

Level 1: (Low) The building the live in has a number of problems. Some of the stairs and the stair railings are loose, there are holes in the ceiling plaster, exposing electrical wires, the bathroom sink is broken and there are several signs of vermin infestation.

Level 2: (High) The building they live in is structurally sound. The stairs, ceilings, walls, and plumbing are in good shape. Occasionally they find some roaches in the apartment.

Dimension 4: Material Goods

Level 1: (Low) (Name) finds she cannot buy a lot of things she feels they need such as a table, beds for the children, cleaning supplies, or common medical supplies such as aspirin. The younger child doesn't have a winter coat. Most of the clothes are second hand and don't fit very well.

Level 2: (Medium) (Name) finds she can afford some of the things they need, but still lacks a living room light, a dresser for the children, and some common medical supplies such as bandaids and aspirin. (name) can buy some of the family's clothes new. Some of the time the children are dressed in clothes that look good and fit well.

Level 3: (High) (Name) finds she can furnish the house with all of the needed furniture. She can almost always buy all the common medical supplies needed. (Name) buys most of the family's clothes new, and the clothing usually looks good and fits well.

Dimension 5: Health Care

Level 1: (Low) Sometimes she doesn't take the children or herself to the doctor when medical attention is needed because (name) feels she can't pay the bill.

Level 2: (High) She always finds a way to take the children or herself to the doctor when needed.

Table 3.2 presents a sample vignette and the rating scales used in the study. After reading each vignette, respondents in the Chicago study were asked to respond to the scenario depicted on each of three scales. In the first scale, respondents were asked "how much of a hardship these conditions create for the (vignette family). Respondents were asked to respond on a scale from 1 (no hardship at all) to 7 (extreme hardship). The second scale asks whether the respondent felt the living conditions of the vignette family were inadequate, adequate or more than adequate.

In the third scale, respondents are informed that the vignette family currently receives a *monthly* AFDC support payment (all vignette families receive $400), and are asked how much money the family "need(s) based on their living conditions described above.." Respondents are then presented a scale marked from 1 to 9 and marked in dollar amounts ranging from $200 (above the 1) to $600 (above the 9). Also, "NO CHANGE" was printed above the $400 mark, with "HIGHER MONTHLY PUBLIC ASSISTANCE PAYMENTS" printed above the higher end of the scale and "LOWER MONTHLY PUBLIC ASSISTANCE PAYMENTS" printed above the lower end of the scale.

The Chicago Study survey also included a brief survey that collected demographic data on respondents, whether the respondent knew persons on AFDC, and four (4) items addressing concerning Aid to Families With Dependent Children (AFDC).

TABLE 3.2 Panel A: The Chicago Study
Sample Vignette and Rating Scale

Lucy Clark and her two children, ages 3 and 6, live in a neighborhood where the roads need repair, but there isn't much litter on the street. It's not the safest neighborhood, but police come quickly when called. The building they live in is structurally sound. The stairs, ceiling, walls, and plumbing are in good shape. Occasionally they find some roaches in the apartment.

Lucy finds she cannot buy a lot of things she feels they need such as a table, beds for the children, cleaning supplies, or common medical supplies such as aspirin. The younger child doesn't have a winter coat. Most of the clothes are second hand and do not fit very well.

In her efforts to make ends meet, Lucy finds that she can always provide three meals a day and enough food for everyone. The children always have milk, but occasionally don't eat meat. Sometimes she doesn't take the children or herself to the doctor when medical attention is needed because Lucy feels she can't pay the bill.

1. In general, how much of a hardship do you think these conditions create for the Clarks?

CIRCLE ONE POSITION

No Hardship At All						Extreme Hardship
1	2	3	4	5	6	7

2. Do you think that the living conditions for the Clark family at this time are more than adequate, adequate, or inadequate?

MORE THAN ADEQUATE	1
ADEQUATE	2
INADEQUATE	3

TABLE 3.2 Panel A: The Chicago Study (continued)
Sample Vignette and Rating Scale

3) The Clark family is currently supported by an AFDC grant of $400. You can INCREASE, DECREASE, OR KEEP THE SAME the monthly payment to the Clark family according to what you feel they **need based on their living conditions described above.**
PLEASE CIRCLE THE NUMBER ON THE LINE WHICH REPRESENTS YOUR DECISION IN THIS CASE ('5' represents the current grant of $400).

(CHANGE IN MONTHLY BENEFIT PAYMENTS)

Lower Monthly Public Assistance Payments			NO Change			Higher Monthly Public Assistance Payments		
$200	$250	$300	$350	$400	$450	$500	$550	$600
1	2	3	4	5	6	7	8	9

THE NEW YORK STUDY: PEREIRA AND ROSSI

The Pereira and Rossi study[3], referred to here as the New York Study, was designed as a pilot study for a nation-wide study of normative views toward welfare entitlements. Because the New York Study was a pilot study, a probability sample of New York residents was not essential. The New York study utilized a block quota design to obtain respondents in order to insure "heterogeneity in socio-economic status and ... provide for spreads in gender and age." (Pereira, p. 18) The New York study data collection was conducted by the National Opinion Research Center, of the University of Chicago, during February and March, 1984. A total of 200 respondents were interviewed.

The New York Study employed a design with 18 dimensions being used in the construction of the vignettes. The New York design allowed for selecting vignette characteristics from all possible characteristics in the full factorial design. The New York Study vignettes were constructed using a computer program that randomly assigned a level of each dimension to the vignette.[4] Each respondent in the New York study was presented with a packet of 51 vignettes. The first vignette was for practice, and was identical for each respondent.

Panel B of Table 3.1 illustrates the dimensions and levels of used in the New York study vignettes. In contrast to the Chicago Study, in which levels within each dimension were several sentences long and contained several pieces of information, the New York study employed dimensions with levels that contained succinct, specific information. Often, levels within a dimension contained only a portion of a sentence. Having multiple dimensions associated with each topic allows for different characteristics of a persons situation to be combined. For example, the vignette characters employment status can address not only whether one is unemployed or not, but also allows for various reasons for a person being unemployed.

In Panel B of Table 3.2, a sample of the vignettes and rating scale used in the New York study is presented. After each vignette, respondents were asked what the vignette character's *weekly* support payment from public agencies should be, given the conditions stated in the vignette. The rating scale consisted of $50 dollar increments, ranging from $0 (labeled no support) to $400 (or more).[5]

After completing the vignette packet, respondents in the New York study filled out a short questionnaire. Respondents were asked basic demographic questions, as well as items concerning their own experience with welfare and the experiences of their family and friends. In addition, scale items dealing with the respondents perceptions toward the treatment of persons in the US were examined.

TABLE 3.1 Panel B: The New York City Study

Dimension 1: SEX OF VIGNETTE PERSON
Level 1: Female (Proper name, 60%)
Level 2: Male (Proper name, 40%)
Dimension 2: RACE
Level 1: White
Level 2: Black
Level 3: Hispanic
Level 4: No Text
Dimension 3: AGE OF REFERENT
Level 1: 16 year old,
Level 2: 18 year old,
Level 3: 21 year old,
Level 4: 24 year old,
Level 5: 26 year old,
Level 6: 29 year old,
Level 7: 32 year old,
Level 8: 35 year old,
Level 9: 41 year old,
Level 10: 45 year old,
Level 11: 48 year old,
Level 12: 51 year old,
Dimension 4: EDUCATION
Level 1: has less than an 8th grade education.
Level 2: has an 8th grade education.
Level 3: completed 2 years of high school.
Level 4: completed 2 years of high school.
Level 5: is a high school graduate.
Level 6: is a high school graduate.
Level 7: completed 2 years of college.
Level 8: is a college graduate.
Dimension 5: MARITAL STATUS
Level 1: Is married and lives with a spouse who works and
Level 2: Is married and lives with a spouse who does not work
Level 3: Lives with a common-law spouse who works and
Level 4: Lives with a common-law spouse who does not work
Level 5: Is married but was deserted by spouse and lives alone

TABLE 3.1 Panel B: The New York City Study (continued)

Dimension 5: MARITAL STATUS (continued)

Level 6: Is separated from spouse and lives alone with

Level 7: Is divorced and lives alone with

Level 8: Is widowed and lives alone with

Level 9: Has never married and lives alone with

Dimension 6: NUMBER OF CHILDREN

Level 1: No children.

Level 2: One child under the age of 12 years.

Level 3: Two children under the age of 12 years.

Level 4: Two children under the age of 12 years.

Level 5: Three children under the age of 12 years.

Level 6: Four children under the age of 12 years.

Dimension 7: EMPLOYMENT STATUS (DISABILITY)

Level 1: is employed (25%)

Level 2: is not working and has never worked (15%)

Level 3: is an unemployed (40%)

Level 4: is an unemployed (20%)

Dimension 8: OCCUPATION

Level 1: car washer

Level 2: construction laborer

Level 3: cook

Level 4: parking lot attendant

Level 5: store clerk

Level 6: assembly line worker

Level 7: car salesperson

Level 8: bus driver

Level 9: cleaning person

Level 10: restaurant worker

Level 11: telephone operator

Level 12: office clerk

Level 13: office manager

Level 14: business manager

Level 15: bookkeeper

Level 16: drill press operator

Level 17: sewing machine operator

Level 18: teacher

Level 19: business owner

TABLE 3.1: Panel B: The New York City Study (continued)
Dimension 9: DISABILITY STATUS FOR EMPLOYED
Level 1: but claims wages are not enough for the family to live
Level 2: claims wages are not enough for a decent life.
Level 3: worried about not having enough free time for family
Level 4: but has many medical bills to pay.
Level 5: and has to provide support for an ex-spouse.
Level 6: and has to provide support for elderly parents.
Level 7: blank text
Dimension 10: DISABILITY FOR NEVER WORKED
Level 1: having been born blind.
Level 2: having been born deaf.
Level 3: having been paralyzed in a childhood accident.
Level 4: because of a physical disability.
Level 5: having been born mentally retarded.
Level 6: having become mentally ill at a young age.
Level 7: having been in prison for some time.
Level 8: having always been supported by parents.
Level 9: having always had to take care of the family.
Level 10: having always had to care for young children.
Dimension 11: DISAB. FOR UNEMPLOYED/LOOKING
Level 1: cannot find a job in that line of work.
Level 2: cannot find a job that pays enough.
Level 3: can only find jobs which require hard and dirty work.
Level 4: does not want to work in a blue collar job.
Level 5: always comes up against job discrimination.
Level 6: is not trained for available jobs.
Level 7: blank text
Dimension 12: DISAB. UNEMPLOYED NOT LOOKING
Level 1: not recovered from a major illness.
Level 2: lost a leg in a job-related accident.
Level 3: permanently disabled after being shot by a policeman.
Level 4: permanently disabled in an assault by an robber.
Level 5: been afflicted with a heart condition.
Level 6: because of a disability incurred during the war.
Level 7: become mentally ill.

TABLE 3.1 Panel B: The New York City Study (continued)

Dimension 12: (continued)
Level 8: depressed/anxious over being unemployed.
Level 9: discouraged over not finding job for two years.
Level 10: need to care for young children.
Level 11: need to care for a handicapped person.
Level 12: don't pay enough to hire someone to care for family.
Level 13: the only jobs available pay too little.
Level 14: the only jobs available involve hard and dirty work.

Dimension 13: REASONS FOR LOSING LAST JOB
Level 1: laid off from last job because company was losing business.
Level 2: lost last job when company went out of business.
Level 3: had to leave last job to undergo surgery.
Level 4: fired from last job for using drugs on the job.
Level 5: fired from last job for drinking alcohol on the job.
Level 6: fired from last job for constantly being late for work.
Level 7: left last job because wages were too low.
Level 8: left last job because children needed care at home.
Level 9: blank text

Dimension 14: NUTRITION/RECREATION
Level 1: usually has 3 meals a day with meat at the main meal.
Level 2: afford to have only 2 meals a day.
Level 3: afford to have 2 meals a day but never a meat dish.
Level 4: afford to only eat poorly and sometimes has to skip the main
    meal.
Level 5: cannot afford to go to the movies once a month.
Level 6: cannot afford to eat out at a family restaurant.
Level 7: cannot afford a television set.
Level 8: can only afford to visit relatives for recreation.
Level 9: cannot afford to have friends over for dinner.
Level 10: cannot afford clothes warm enough for the winter.
Level 11: cannot afford to have a telephone.
Level 12: blank text (4 Levels)

TABLE 3.1 Panel B: The New York City Study (continued)

Dimension 15: HOUSING CONDITION

Level 1: maintained and comfortable in the winter/summer.
Level 2: broken windows, poor plumbing and exposed wiring.
Level 3: place that gets very little heat in the winter.
Level 4: no hot water/heat & is infested with rats and roaches.
Level 5: everyone in the family has their own bedroom.
Level 6: all members of the family share the same bedroom.
Level 7: can only afford one bed for all the children.
Level 8: have to use the living room as a sleeping area.
Level 9: can afford only one bedroom for all the children.
Level 10: blank text

Dimension 16: HOUSING EXPENSES

$25 increments from $50 to $250, and $290, $330, and $400.

Dimension 17: INCOME LEVELS

Level 1: $ 50 per week (2 Levels)
Level 2: $ 70 per week
Level 3: $ 90 per week (2 Levels)
Level 4: $110 per week (2 Levels)
Level 5: $130 per week (2 Levels)
Level 6: $150 per week
Level 7: $170 per week
Level 8: $190 per week
Level 9: $210 per week
Level 10: $275 per week
Level 11: $355 per week
Level 12: $435 per week
Level 13: $ 0 per week

TABLE 3.1 Panel B: The New York City Study (continued)
Dimension 18: GOVERNMENT SUPPORT
Level 1: $ 0 per week (3 Levels)
Level 2: $ 10 per week (2 Levels)
Level 3: $ 20 per week (2 Levels)
Level 4: $ 30 per week (2 Levels)
Level 5: $ 40 per week (2 Levels)
Level 6: $ 50 per week (2 Levels)
Level 7: $ 60 per week
Level 8: $ 70 per week
Level 9: $ 80 per week
Level 10: $ 90 per week
Level 11: $100 per week
Level 12: $120 per week
Level 13: $150 per week
Level 14: $210 per week
Level 15: $250 per week
Level 16: $300 per week
Level 17: $360 per week

TABLE 3.2 Panel B: The New York City Study
Sample Vignette and Rating Scale

Mary R., A White, 32 year old, has less than an 8th grade education. She is married and lives with a spouse who does not work and three children under the age of 12 years.

She is an unemployed assembly line worker and is not looking for work because the only jobs available involve hard and dirty work. She had to leave her last job to undergo surgery.

The family claims it can afford to have only 2 meals a day.
The family pays $400 a month for housing.

Take home wages of family members	$ 0 per week.
Support payment from public agencies	$ 90 per week.
Total Family Income	$ 90

What do you think the support payment from public agencies should be?

$0--$50--$100--$150--$200--$250--$300--$350--$400
No   Or
Support   More

THE GENERAL SOCIAL SURVEY VIGNETTE STUDY

The General Social Survey (GSS) is a national probability sample survey conducted each year[6] by the National Opinion Research Center at the University of Chicago. In the 1986 survey, both conventional survey items dealing with perceptions of the welfare recipients and a supplemental factorial survey section were employed to address perceptions concerning what characterizes those persons who are deserving of welfare assistance.

The GSS vignette component was in part a product of the New York Study vignettes. Several important changes were made in the design of these vignettes, with some dimensions and levels used in the New York study remaining in the GSS design, some dimensions being dropped, and some additional dimensions included. In addition, because of time constraints imposed by the nature of the GSS, the number of vignettes was reduced from 50 to 10 vignettes per respondent.

Panel C of Table 3.1 presents the dimensions and levels used in the GSS study. As can be seen in the tables, the number of dimensions in the GSS vignettes is reduced from the 18 dimensions used in the New York study to 11. Also, note that in addition to the young family scenarios, additional vignettes concerning old women were included. In the vignettes depicting old women, a total of 5 dimensions were included. In all, each respondent was presented with 10 vignettes, 7 associated with young families and 3 associated with old women.

In order to facilitate the methodological comparisons of these studies, only those General Social Survey vignettes dealing with the young families will be used here. Neither of the other studies discussed above dealt with vignette characters older than age 51 (age was not included in the Chicago study at all). Therefore, direct comparison is not possible.

TABLE 3.1 Panel C: The GSS Young Family Vignettes
Vignette Dimensions and Levels

Dimension 1: NUMBER OF CHILDREN
Level 1: one six month old child
Level 2: one four year old child
Level 3: one eight year old child
Level 4: two children, the youngest is six months old
Level 5: two children, the youngest is four years old
Level 6: two children, the youngest is eight years old
Level 7: four children, the youngest is six months old
Level 8: four children, the youngest is four years old
Level 9: four children, the youngest is eight years old

Dimension 2: MARITAL STATUS
Level 1: the parents are married.
Level 2: the mother is divorced.
Level 3: the mother never married.

Dimension 3: SITUATION OF THE CHILD'S FATHER
Level 1: is employed full time.
Level 2: is unemployed but looking for work.
Level 3: is unemployed and not looking for work.
Level 4: is currently in prison.
Level 5: is permanently disabled.

Dimension 4: CHILD'S MOTHER'S EDUCATION
Level 1: a grade school education and is
Level 2: some high school education and is
Level 3: a high school education and is
Level 4: some college education and is
Level 5: has a college degree and is

TABLE 3.1 Panel C: The GSS Vignettes (continued)
Vignette Dimensions and Levels

Dimension 6 MOTHER'S EMPLOYMENT STATUS
Level 1: working full time.
Level 2: working part time.
Level 3: looking for work.
Level 4: unemployed and not looking for work.
Level 5: unemployed and not looking for work because she can't find affordable daycare.
Level 6: unemployed and not looking for work because she has no ready means of transportation.
Level 7: unemployed and not looking for work because the available jobs only pay the minimum wage.
Level 8: blank text
Dimension 7: MARITAL STATUS OF THE FATHER
Level 1: the father has remarried and
Level 2: blank text
Dimension 8: FINANCIAL PROSPECTS
Level 1: financial difficulties only for the next six months.
Level 2: financial difficulties for a couple of years.
Level 3: financial difficulties continually in the future.
Dimension 9: DO HER PARENTS HELP
Level 1: help out financially.
Level 2: cannot help out financially.
Level 3: could help out financially but she won't ask.
Level 4: could help out financially but they refuse.
Dimension 10: SAVINGS
Level 1: has no savings. (75%)
Level 2: has $1000 in savings. (25%)
Dimension 11: TOTAL FAMILY INCOME
Level 1: $50 per week.
Level 2: $100 per week.
Level 3: $200 per week.
Level 4: $300 per week.

In Panel C of Table 3.2, a sample vignette and the accompanying rating scale from the GSS are presented. The rating scale for the GSS vignettes consisted of $50 dollar increments, ranging from $0 to $600. The current family income of the family portrayed in the vignette was labeled above the appropriate position on the rating scale. Also, each scale identified the average U.S. family income above the $400 position. Respondents were asked to indicate "What should this family's weekly income be? Include amounts ... sources other than government and any public assistance...".

TABLE 3.2 Panel C: The GSS Study
Sample Vignette and Rating Scale

This family has four children, the youngest is six months old, living with their mother. The mother is divorced. The mother has a college degree and is unemployed and not looking for work because she has no ready means of transportation. The father has remarried and is permanently disabled. The family is likely to face financial difficulties for a couple of years. Her parents cannot help out financially. The family has $1000 in savings. All in all, the family's total income from sources other than the government is $100 per week.

What should this family's weekly income be? Include both the money already available from sources other than the government, and any public assistance support you think this family should get.

```
Amount already received      Average U.S.
     by this family          Family Income
          X                       X
$/WEEK|__|__|__|__|__|__|__|__|__|__|__|__|
      0   50  100 150 200 250 300 350 400 450 500 550 600
```

As stated above, the General Social Survey is a yearly national survey and covers many diverse topics each year. The entire survey is quite extensive, and the vignette supplement was only a small part of the entire project. Also included in the 1986 survey, however, was a battery of questions addressing the respondents' attitudes toward people on welfare and the effect welfare has on recipients. For the purposes of this study, a portion of the overall survey, including the battery of questions mentioned above, demographic characteristics of the respondents, and political affiliation and attitude items were extracted from the overall survey.

DISTRIBUTIONS OF GENEROSITY
A cursory examination and comparison of the rating scales used in these studies shows the scales to be quite similar. In each of the studies, a scale using dollar increments was used.[7] Also, each rating scale indicated the current amount of support the vignette family received--a constant $400 for the Chicago Study vignette family and a floating amount for the New York and GSS studies.

On closer examination, however, several important differences in the scales are evident. First, as can be seen in Table 3.2, although each of the studies use a rating scale with increments to $600 (the New York study used both a $400 maximum and a $600 maximum scale), other aspects of the scales were quite different. For example, note that the Chicago study scale did not extend below the $200 allotment (a '1' on the 9 point scale), whereas both the New York and the GSS studies allowed for ratings as low as $0. Second, unlike the New York Study and the GSS, which ask respondents for a weekly cash entitlement rating, the Chicago study vignette rating asks respondents for a MONTHLY AFDC allotment. Also, whereas the Chicago study and the New York study directly ask what amount of Public Assistance the respondent feels the vignette character should get (AFDC for Chicago, and "Support Payments from Public Agencies" for New York), the GSS asks what the vignette family's weekly INCOME should be--from all sources, public and money already available from other sources.

With these differences in structure of the rating scales used in these studies kept in mind, a comparison of the overall levels of generosity toward the vignette characters is possible. In Table 3.3, the distribution of the rating scales from each of the three studies is presented.

Generosity in Chicago.

In Panel A of Table 3.3, the three rating scales used in the Chicago study are presented. For the first two rating scales, the degree of hardship and the adequacy of the living conditions, responses are somewhat skewed toward the high end, indicating perceptions of more extreme levels of hardship and less than adequate living conditions for the vignette family. More than 55 percent of the responses to the vignettes in the Chicago study indicated that the situation portrayed showed inadequate living conditions. In addition, almost 30 percent of the responses on the hardship rating indicated extreme, or nearly extreme hardship. Note also, however, that in approximately 6 percent of the vignette scenarios the living conditions were considered "more than adequate," and in more than 42 percent of the vignettes the living conditions were considered to be adequate or better. In almost 14 percent of the scenarios respondents perceived virtually no hardship, with more than 30 percent of the vignette ratings falling on the "little or no hardship" end of the scale. It appears, therefore, that although none of the dimensions and levels depicted in the vignettes could be said to indicate true "well being" for the vignette characters, not all of the situations elicited equal amounts of sympathy from respondents.

The third rating for the Chicago study, the amount of AFDC support that was considered to be needed, was not as drastically skewed as the hardship and adequacy scales. Overall, in almost 72 percent of the vignette scenarios the suggested AFDC grant fell in the middle categories between $400 and $500.

In almost 24 percent of the vignettes in the Chicago study, the AFDC grant suggested by respondents equaled the $400 amount the vignette family already received. In slightly more than 6 percent of the cases, the AFDC benefit proposed represented a cut in already existing awards. In almost 14 percent of the vignettes, the AFDC grant awarded was $600, the maximum amount listed on the scale. No vignette scenarios were awarded an AFDC grant less than $250.

TABLE 3.3 Panel A: The Chicago Study
Vignette Scale Responses

1) HOW MUCH HARDSHIP?

		%	cum %
NO HARDSHIP	1	4.4	4.4
	2	9.2	13.6
	3	17.2	30.8
	4	17.7	48.5
	5	21.9	70.4
	6	13.8	84.2
EXTREME HARDSHIP	7	15.8	100.0

Mean   4.48   Median   3.0   N =   993

2) LIVING CONDITIONS

		%	cum%
MORE THAN	1	5.7	5.7
ADEQUATE	2	36.5	42.2
INADEQUATE	3	57.8	100.0

Mean   2.52   Median   5.0   N =   992

3) AFDC GRANT NEEDED PER MONTH

Amount	%	cum %
$250	.2	.2
$300	2.3	2.5
$350	3.6	6.1
$400	23.9	30.1
$450	22.5	52.6
$500	25.3	77.9
$550	8.2	86.1
$600	13.9	100.0

Scale Mean   6.5   Median   6.0   N = 995
Dollar Mean[8] $472.26   Median $450.00

When adjusting the AFDC grant amount awarded by the respondents by the amount of AFDC already received by the vignette family, we find that only in a small percent of the cases was there a rating that would lower benefits. Panel A of Table 3.4 illustrates the distribution of the "Net Benefits" for the Chicago study. This table was constructed by subtracting the AFDC grant currently received by the vignette family (in the Chicago study all awards were $400) from the rating amount awarded to each vignette by respondents. Again, as can be seen in this table the large majority of vignettes awards would either keep the current level of support the same or award small increases of $50 to $100.

For the most part, therefore, no desire for drastic changes in the monthly AFDC grant, whether increasing or decreasing the amount already granted, is shown in the distribution of the AFDC award rating. Overall responses to the vignettes, irrespective of the various dimensions and levels within each scenario, suggested either no change in AFDC award or only modest increases of $50 to $100 per month ($0 to $25 per week) were warranted.

TABLE 3.4 Panel A: The Chicago Study
Net Benefit For Vignette Awards[9]

Net Benefits	%
-150.00	.2
-100.00	2.3
-50.00	3.6
0.00	23.9
50.00	22.5
100.00	25.3
150.00	8.2
200.00	13.9

Valid Cases   995

Generosity in New York.

As can be seen in Panel B of Table 3.3, the New York study vignette rating distribution contains a large amount of variation. Although the rating scale was marked for responses in $50 increments, the dashes between each of the marked points on the scale served as $10 interval marks during the rating process. (See Table 3.2) Despite this large variation in the vignette rating, however, most responses to the vignettes clustered around the $50 interval marks. Note, again, that the New York rating represents respondents perception of the amount of public assistance vignette characters should receive *PER WEEK.*

Examination of the New York Rating reveals some important characteristics of the levels of generosity within the New York sample and some differences with the Chicago study. First, note that the modal public assistance award given by the sample was $0. In all, more than 1400 responses, or 14 percent, indicated that the vignette characters deserved *NO* weekly support from public agencies. An additional 12 percent of the vignette ratings fell at or less than $50 in public support per week; a total of 26 percent at or below the $50 mark. The average award given in the New York study vignettes was over $156 per week, with the median award being almost $150 per week. Despite the addition of the $600 maximum scale, less than .01 percent of the vignette ratings awarded more than the original maximum of $400 per week. Slightly more than 10 percent of the vignette responses awarded over $300 per week to the vignette characters.

Generosity displayed by the awards granted on the New York City vignettes, as seen in the basic distribution of awards, reveals much less overall structure than the Chicago study displayed. With the exception, albeit an important one, of the large number of vignette scenarios awarded $0 in support, public assistance awards are approximately normally distributed.

TABLE 3.3 Panel B: The New York City Study
Vignette Scale Responses

Weekly Income Award Given

$ VALUE	FREQ	PCT	$VALUE	FREQ	PCT	$VALUE	FREQ	PCT
.00	1409	14	140.00	38	0	285.00	11	0
5.00	20	0	145.00	11	0	290.00	7	0
10.00	54	1	150.00	1051	11	295.00	50	0
13.00	1	0	155.00	31	0	300.00	616	6
15.00	27	0	160.00	46	0	305.00	5	0
20.00	110	1	165.00	31	0	310.00	15	0
25.00	77	1	170.00	82	1	315.00	9	0
30.00	83	1	175.00	85	1	320.00	40	0
35.00	15	0	180.00	58	1	325.00	39	0
40.00	63	1	185.00	14	0	330.00	29	0
45.00	28	0	190.00	27	0	335.00	3	0
50.00	669	7	195.00	10	0	340.00	10	0
55.00	11	0	200.00	1103	11	345.00	5	0
60.00	46	0	205.00	13	0	350.00	312	3
65.00	20	0	210.00	84	1	355.00	6	0
70.00	89	1	215.00	34	0	360.00	29	0
75.00	44	0	220.00	59	1	365.00	25	0
80.00	88	1	225.00	35	0	370.00	24	0
85.00	19	0	230.00	29	0	375.00	36	0
90.00	78	1	235.00	12	0	380.00	32	0
95.00	22	0	240.00	17	0	385.00	10	0
100.00	998	10	245.00	2	0	390.00	14	0
105.00	14	0	250.00	687	7	395.00	4	0
110.00	45	0	255.00	3	0	400.00	373	4
115.00	44	0	260.00	23	0	500.00	14	0
120.00	114	1	265.00	23	0	550.00	1	0
125.00	81	1	270.00	39	0	600.00	5	0
130.00	58	1	275.00	38	0			
135.00	14	0	280.00	14	0			

MEAN $156.67   MEDIAN $149.89

N =   9819

When examining the "Net Benefits" awarded in the New York Study, however, several distinct patterns emerge. In the New York study, overall family income included two components: the income amount the vignette family currently received from non-government sources, and the amount of public assistance received. Therefore, two versions of "Net Benefit" amount can be looked at here. First, we subtracted the total family income (income from other sources combined with the public assistance received) from the rating given to the vignette. Second, we subtracted the current amount of public assistance received by the vignette family from the amount of assistance given in the vignette rating. In Panel B1 and B2 of Table 3.4 the distributions of the two Net Benefit measures for the New York Study are presented.

When examining the differences between the amount of total family income and the Public Assistance award, vignette character families do not fare very well. As can be seen in Panel B1, 43 percent of the ratings actually served to reduce the weekly income of the vignette families. Twenty seven percent of these reductions totalled $100 or more. In addition, another 5 percent of the vignette ratings resulted in no change overall for the vignette family income. Overall, the average vignette award only increased the vignette family's total weekly income by $1.31.

When examining the change in overall Public Assistance award, however, the picture was not quite as drastic. When comparing the differences between current and proposed public assistance award, only 26 percent of the vignette ratings represented a decrease in the overall public assistance award. Another 9 percent of the responses indicated no change in benefits. A little more than 10 percent of the responses "awarded" a $100 or more decrease in public assistance of per week.

Thus it appears that the level of generosity, as shown in the overall level of public assistance awards, is somewhat low. Vignette family incomes, without taking into account the situational components of each vignette, are felt to be adequate, and that primarily small increases, if not actual decreases in weekly income are all that are warranted.

**TABLE 3.4 Panel B: The New York City Study
Net Benefit For Vignette Awards**

Net Benefits	%	Cum %
-600.00	2.2	2.2
-500.00	.8	3.0
-400.00	2.6	5.6
-350.00	1.9	7.5
-345.00	.2	7.7
-300.00	1.8	9.4
-250.00	2.8	12.2
-200.00	3.8	16.0
-150.00	5.7	21.7
-100.00	6.2	28.0
-50.00	8.0	36.0
-1.00	7.6	43.6
.00	5.3	48.9
50.00	11.3	60.2
100.00	11.1	71.4
150.00	8.9	80.3
200.00	7.7	88.0
250.00	4.7	92.6
300.00	3.5	96.2
350.00	2.1	98.3
400.00	1.6	99.9
450.00	.0	99.9
500.00	.1	100.0
600.00	.0	100.0

MEAN   1.310   MEDIAN   10.000

N = 9719

Generosity in the GSS National Sample.

Unlike the New York study, which was used as its pilot study, the GSS vignette study used a less "open" interval scale, guiding responses to $50 increment marks rather than allowing for the $5 and $10 increments. In Panel C of Table 3.3, the distribution of the weekly income award given to the vignette family in the GSS vignettes is presented. Note, again, that unlike the Chicago study and the New York study, the GSS vignettes asked what the vignette family should have for a weekly INCOME, not only what amount of public support should be given. Here it is only implied in the instructions for the vignettes that increases in weekly income could "lead to changes in the taxes we pay."

TABLE 3.3 Panel C: The GSS Study[10]
Vignette Scale Responses

Weekly Income Award	%	cum
0	2.1	2.1
50	3.0	5.1
100	8.3	13.4
150	6.3	19.7
200	20.0	39.7
250	10.9	50.6
300	28.5	79.1
350	7.6	86.7
400	9.0	95.7
450	2.0	97.7
500	1.5	99.2
550	.3	99.4
600	.6	100.0

MEAN   255.856   MEDIAN   250.000   VALID N 9537

As can be seen in Table 3.3, almost 50 percent of the responses to the GSS vignettes fell at or between the $200 and $300 weekly income level. Both the mean income level (just over $255) and the median income level ($250) fall in the center of this range. In contrast to the New York Study, where more that 14 percent of the vignette responses were $0, only 2 percent of the GSS vignettes received a $0 weekly income rating. In addition, only 2.3 percent of the vignettes were considered to be deserving of a weekly income over $450. Only 14.3 percent of the responses awarded a $400 or greater weekly income, suggesting only minimal effect was made by having the "Average Family Income" marked on the scale at the $400 mark.

Examination of Panel C of Table 3.4, however, reveals a striking pattern in the overall estimation of the Vignette family's needed weekly income. When calculating the "Net Benefits" awarded to the vignette characters (the total vignette family income subtracted from the proposed income given by respondents in the vignette rating) the generosity of respondents becomes less clear. That is, holding constant the situational characteristics presented in the vignette scenario, most of the family incomes portrayed in the vignettes were considered adequate. In more than one third of all vignettes (37.3 percent) the proposed income given in the rating for the vignette family did not change from what was presented in the vignettes. In more than 6 percent of the scenarios, the vignettes elicited a rating that would decrease the weekly family income of the vignette characters. In addition, another 28.5 percent of the responses to the vignettes proposed a $100 or less increase in weekly income. Overall, the mean proposed vignette income increased only $74.87.

TABLE 3.4 Panel C: The GSS Study
Net Benefit For Vignette Awards

Net Benefits	%	Cum %
-300	1.1	1.1
-250	.3	1.3
-200	1.1	2.5
-150	.7	3.2
-100	1.6	4.8
-50	1.5	6.3
0	37.3	43.6
50	11.8	55.3
100	16.7	72.0
150	9.1	81.2
200	9.0	90.1
250	3.8	93.9
300	3.3	97.2
350	1.5	98.7
400	.7	99.5
450	.3	99.7
500	.2	99.9
550	.1	100.0

MEAN   74.866   MEDIAN   50.000

VALID N = 9537

WHAT CONDITIONS AFFECT GENEROSITY?

The levels of generosity toward the poor discussed above, while important for general understanding of the levels of public assistance support, does not allow us to separate the *conditions* under which generosity increases or decreases. Basic distributions within such scales can best be understood by examining the separate effects of the various components, or dimensions, of the scenario, and the change in generosity through various degrees, or levels, of these dimensions. The factorial survey design, by randomizing the inclusion of various levels and dimensions, allows us to examine these effects more closely through multiple regression analysis techniques.

For each of the studies examined here, we used multiple regression analysis regressing the individual vignette ratings against each level of each dimension. For "quantitative" dimensions, for example, number of children or age, the dimension was recoded to represent the precise value (e.g. respondent age was recoded so that the variable value equalled the person's age in years). For categorical, or "qualitative" dimensions, a dummy variable was created for each level of the dimension, with one level being omitted to serve as a reference point for the analysis. For example, work status dimensions with 4 levels would be represented by 3 dummy variables (e.g. one each for unemployed-looking, unemployed-not looking, and never worked), with the fourth level (e.g. currently employed) being omitted for reference purposes. In Table 3.5, the results of the regression models for each of the three studies are presented.

Changes in Generosity: Chicago.

Although the dimensions and levels used in the Chicago study were described as being degrees of well being for that issue, the amount and variety of information provided in each level required that these dimensions be examined as categorical, or qualitative. Dummy variables were created for each of the "medium" and "low" levels in the dimensions, with the "high" level being used as the reference for the analysis. In Panel A of Table 3.5, the results of the Chicago regression is are presented. In this table, note that for the Hardship scale and the Adequacy scale, a higher number represents an overall decrease in quality. Thus a "3" on the adequacy scale represent inadequate conditions were perceived, and a "7" on the Hardship scale indicates extreme hardship.

When comparing the level of hardship perceived and the adequacy of the vignette characters living conditions, we find that for each of these scales all of the dimensions have a significant effect on the overall rating. On the "hardship" rating, when compared to those vignettes depicting "high" quality of each of the dimensions, the "low quality" category for each dimension increases the perceptions of hardship, with significance levels of .001 for all of the levels except poor health care. For those vignettes in which the family experiences poor health care, the hardship rating increase is significant at $p < .05$, easily past acceptable reporting levels. The Adequacy of Conditions scale is quite similar. Here, 5 of the 8 dummy variable coefficients are significant at .001, and only the coefficient for medium nutrition fails to meet the $p < .05$ standard. The medium food quality coefficient is, however, significant at $p < .001$.

For all vignettes that depict medium or low levels within any of the dimensions, a significant increase in the perceptions of difficulty for the vignette family is found for both the hardship and the adequacy rating. Vignettes depicting the worst levels of household goods and nutrition quality have the strongest effect on the hardship rating, increasing perceptions of hardship by 1.2 and .93 points (on the 7 point scale) respectively. Low neighborhood quality increased the hardship rating by .79. As can be seen by examining the R^2, almost 15 percent of the variance in the hardship rating can be explained by the vignette dimensions, irrespective of any respondent characteristics.

The largest dimension level effects on the Adequacy scale were low housing quality (.41), low neighborhood quality (.37), and low quality of household goods (.32), again, all of which are significant at $p > .001$. In addition, as can be seen by the R^2 value, approximately 18 percent of the variance in this scale can be explained by these dimensions and levels.

TABLE 3.5 Panel A: The Chicago Study
Vignette Rating Regression
Primary Dimensions and Levels

	Benefits[11] B	Hardship B	Adequacy B
Neighborhood Quality (High Quality omitted)			
bad neighborhood	24.26***	.79***	.37***
neighborhood ok	15.09*	.48***	.21***
Housing Quality (High Quality omitted)			
housing worst	14.29**	.55***	.41***
Household Goods Quality (High Quality omitted)			
worst household goods	39.13***	1.20***	.32***
ok household goods	16.38*	.57***	.19***
Nutrition Quality (High Quality omitted)			
worst nutrition	25.97***	.93***	.15**
medium nutrition	14.43*	.46***	.09#
Health Care Quality (High Quality omitted)			
worst health care	9.46#	.27*	.08*
Constant	413.98***	2.58***	1.86***
R Square	.073	.154	.185
Adjusted R Square	.066	.147	.179
N	994	992	991

\# = $p < .10$
* = $p < .05$
** = $p < .01$
*** = $p < .001$
**** = $p < .0001$

When examining the Benefit rating scale and the amount of AFDC awarded to the vignette families, the overall effect of the vignette dimensions and levels is not as great as found with the hardship and adequacy scales. This is not to say that no effect was detected, for all but one of the coefficients from the dimension levels were significant at p < .05. What is of interest here is the dramatic decrease in the explanatory power of the dimensions and levels when comparing the hardship and adequacy ratings with the benefits awarded. Overall, only 7 percent (R^2 = .073) of the overall variance in the benefit rating could be explained by the dimensions and levels in the vignettes. In addition, of the 8 levels of dimensions used in the equation, only 4 of the variables elicited a significant increase the benefit rating where p < .01 (versus 6 and 7 levels, respectively in the adequacy and hardship ratings).

The transformation of the 9-point rating scale allows us to discuss the results of the regression with the benefit scale in dollars. For example, when examining the coefficients for vignettes depicting the worst neighborhood conditions, we find that, when compared to vignettes with a high quality situation, respondents awarded an additional $24.26 in AFDC benefits to the vignette family. When the vignette family had the worst quality of household goods, the average AFDC award increased by $39.13 per month (p < .001).

When examining the dimensions and levels used in the Chicago study vignettes and the effect these dimensions and levels have on the various ratings, several findings stand out. First, almost every dimension and level for each of the rating scales had a significant impact on the respondents' judgments (p < .05 or greater). Second, examination of the changes in the coefficients from each of the equations reveals that the changes in the situations within the vignette scenarios *does* affect the respondents' perceptions of difficulty. In every case, a decrease in the relative quality of the dimension in question (e.g. neighborhood quality, nutrition quality, etc.), elicited an increase in each of the rating scales, and an increase in the proposed cash benefits. Finally, whereas it appears that there is a great deal of agreement among the respondents as to the level of hardship endured, and the extent to which conditions are inadequate, given the vignette scenario, such agreement is less pronounced when allocating additional resources to AFDC recipients. Despite the appearance of hardship and inadequate living conditions, whether one is entitled to additional benefits is less clear when examining the situational makeup of the vignette family.

Changes in Generosity: New York City.

The dimensions used in constructing the vignettes for the New York study included both quantitative and qualitative levels. When regressing the Total Public Assistance award (award rating) against the dimensions and levels from the vignette, the characters' age, highest grade in school completed (education), number of children in the vignette family, and the "cash flow" dimensions (rent paid, income received, and current government support) were used as continuous variables. Dummy variables were created from the levels of the categorical vignette dimensions, with one level of each dimension being omitted for reference purposes. In Panel B of table 3.5, the results from the New York study regression are presented.[12]

Note that, by having the rating scale in whole dollar increments, the regression coefficients can be seen as dollar amount increases or decreases. When regressing the amount of public assistance awarded against the vignette characteristics, without including any respondent characteristics, we are able to explain slightly more than 11 percent of the variation in the award rating.

Several dimensions included in the New York study vignettes appeared to have virtually no effect on the level of support awarded to vignette family. The age and education of the vignette character have almost no impact on the weekly public assistance grant awarded to the vignettes, and the race of the vignette character has only a small (and not significant at $p < .05$) increase in the total award.

The gender of the vignette character also has only a small impact on the award rating. However, note that for vignettes where the vignette character is male, the average public assistance award was $4.30 more than if the vignette character was female ($p < .1$). Although this increase is small, and not significant to the .05 cutoff being used here, that there is even this much of an increase seems counter-intuitive. Folk wisdom would believe female characters with children have and advantage, as they would be perceived to be less capable of managing without assistance than a male (who presumably would have more opportunity to find gainful employment).

TABLE 3.5 Panel B: The New York City Study
Vignette Rating Regression
Primary Dimensions and Levels

	B
Gender of Vignette Character (Female omitted)	
Male vignette person	4.30#
Race of vignette character (blank text omitted)	
White	2.95
Black	4.55
Hispanic	2.75
Age of vignette character (continuous)	
Age in vignette	.14
Education of vignette character (continuous)	
Education in vignette	-.11
Marital status of vignette character (never married omitted)	
Married-spouse works	-1.30
Married-spouse unemployed	-12.00**
Common law-spouse unemployed	-10.71*
Common law-spouse works	.19
Deserted by spouse	3.89
Separated	5.12
Divorced	-4.38
Widowed	-.67
Number of kids in vignette (continuous)	
Number of children in vignette	22.17***
Employment status (never worked omitted)	
Employed	-9.67*
Unemployed and looking	-12.09***
Unemployed and not looking	-6.74#

TABLE 3.5 Panel B: The New York City Study (continued)
Vignette Rating Regression

	B
Nutrition and recreation (no text omitted)	
3 meals daily with meat	-3.33
Meals daily	.32
No meat but 2 meals daily	3.94
Eat poorly & skip main meal	2.94
Cant afford monthly movies	-6.65
Cant afford restaurant	-1.51
Cant afford a television	.29
Can afford visiting relatives	-1.34
Cant afford friends at dinner	-11.14*
Cant afford winter cloths	-2.98#
Cant afford a telephone	2.65
Housing conditions (no text omitted)	
Well maintained place	-9.04*
Broken windows,poor plumbing	6.14
Little heat in winter	2.51
No heat or hot water,rats	-.06
Everyone has own bedroom	-8.76*
All share the same bdrm	-3.31
One bed for all the kids	2.41
Living room used for sleeping	5.05
One bedroom for all children	1.86
Expenditures (continuous)	
Rent -amount spent on housing	.048***
Cash received - sources (continuous)	
Earnings-take home wages of family	-.21***
Amount of support payment from govt	.13***
(Constant)	109.25***

R Square	.117	
Adjusted R Square	.114	
N = 9718		
# = p < .10	*** = p < .001	
* = p < .05	**** = p < .0001	
** = p < .01		

Several other dimensions used in the New York Study had "mixed" effects on the public assistance award given to the vignettes. That is, several dimensions had one or more levels that had a significant effect on changes in the rating, but only some of the levels were significant. When examining the vignette characters marital status, for example, we find that for most of the status possibilities the amount of public assistance awarded was not significantly affected. For two levels of the marital status dimension, however, respondents penalized the vignette family. If the vignette family had two adults in the house--whether married or "common-law"--and the spouse was not working, the vignette family's average public assistance award was *decreased*. If the vignette character was married and the spouse was unemployed, the average award decreased by $12.00 per week (p < .01). If the spouse was "common-law", the average award decreased by $10.71 per week (p < .05). However, if the couple was married and the spouse worked, the average rating decreased only $1.30 per week, and the average award for common law couples where the spouse was working increased slightly (neither of these coefficients was significant, even at p < .10).

Two dimensions in the New York study vignettes, the nutrition and recreation dimension and the housing condition dimension, also had only particular levels which were significant. Average public assistance awards for vignette families with housing conditions where the residence was well maintained, or those families that had separate bedrooms for everyone decrease by approximately $9 per week ($9.04 and $8.76 respectively p < .05), compared to those vignettes where housing condition was unknown. For those vignette families where the primary nutrition-recreation "complaint" was the inability to have friends over for dinner, the average weekly assistance was *decreased* more than $11 per week (p < .05). Public assistance awards to vignette families where the family's concern is the inability to afford movies decreased an average of $6.65. Those families with adequate living conditions and those whose "complaints" are less central to maintaining the basic necessities are seen as less deserving than those who live in less satisfactory conditions.

In contrast to the variables previously discussed, several dimensions strongly affect the amount of public assistance awarded to the vignette families: one qualitative, or categorical, dimension employment status of the vignette character; and four quantitative, or continuous, dimensions, number of children, and the fixed expenditures variables (rent paid per month, family income and government support already received).

As can be seen in Panel B, one of the more dramatic characteristics for determining the amount of public assistance awarded to the vignette family is the number of children in that family. For each additional child portrayed in the vignette scenario, an average of $22.17 is added to the proposed award (p < .001). For vignette families with four children, this would amount to an increase of almost $90 per week. The amount of rent paid by the vignette family, and the weekly family income are also particularly important in determining the level of public assistance awarded to the family. For each dollar of *monthly* rent paid by the vignette character, an additional $.05 per week is awarded in public assistance payments (p < .001). However, when examining the effect of the vignette characters' weekly income, we find that for every dollar of income, the average public assistance award is reduced by $.21.

The dummy variables created from the current work status of the vignette character elicited strong punitive reaction. When compared to those people who had never worked, those vignettes in which the vignette character was employed, vignettes where the character was unemployed an looking for work, and those in which the character was unemployed and not looking all received significantly lower public assistance awards. Vignette characters who were unemployed, yet looking for work, received the largest cut, averaging more than $12 per week less than those who never worked (p < .001). The average assistance awarded for persons who were employed was almost $10 less than those who never worked, while those persons who were unemployed and not looking averaged $6.74 less than those who never worked. Even more interesting, and somewhat counterintuitive, is the effect of the amount of current public assistance currently being received by the vignette family. For each dollar of government assistance received by the vignette family, the average assistance awarded by respondents increased by $.13 (p < .001).

Thus, without taking into account the reasons why the vignette character was not looking for work or had never worked, it appears that those with some advantage (i.e. are already employed, or are

unemployed but attempting to change the situation) deserve less
public assistance than those vignette characters who are "out of it"
and appear on the surface to be somewhat incapable of adequately
helping themselves. Since they have already been deemed needy of
some (increasing) level of aid, people already receiving public
assistance, and people who appear to be incapable of helping
themselves also receive additional compensation as the amount of
assistance previously awarded increases.

Changing Generosity in the Nation: The GSS Vignettes.
      The GSS study vignettes, like the New York study, contained
both quantitative and qualitative dimensions. In addition, one
dimension, the number and age of children, was transformed into two
separate variables, one each for the age and number of children. The
education of the vignette family mother, the family savings, and the
weekly family income all were used as continuous variables. Dummy
variables were created for each of the levels for the remaining
dimensions: mothers' and fathers' marital status, fathers employment
situation, mothers' employment status, future financial prospects and
the parental help dimensions. In Panel C of Table 3.5 the results of
the regression for the GSS vignette dimensions and levels on the
amount awarded are presented. The design of the GSS vignette rating
allows us to interpret the regression coefficients as direct increases in
the dollar amount of the award rating.
      As can be seen in Panel C, two dimensions, the marital status of
both the mother and the father of the vignette family, had no
significant effect on the amount of income awarded by respondents.
Two other dimensions, the vignette family's future financial prospects
and the extent of the vignette characters' parental help, had only a
minimal effect. Those families facing financial problems for "the next
few years" received slightly less than 5 percent per week in additional
income ($p < .10$). Those vignette families where the parents were
willing to help the family out financially, but the vignette family
mother would not ask, were slightly penalized, receiving an average
of $4.70 less than those whose parents currently helped out ($p < .10$).
      The employment characteristics of both of the vignette family
parents proved to have a strong effect on the overall income rating
given by GSS respondents. Of particular importance is the dimension
addressing the current situation of the father in the vignette. For

those families where the father was disabled and thus unable to provide substantial support for the family, the average income rating was more than $26 higher than for those families where the father worked (p < .001). Vignettes where the father was unemployed, yet looking for work, the average income rating increased by more than $12 over families with an employed father (p < .001). Unemployed fathers who were not looking for work were penalized $7.13 per week (p < .05), yet families where the father was in prison were given slightly higher weekly income ratings (p < .10).

When examining the effect of the mothers education and employment status, respondents appear more punitive. For the mothers, each year of education increases the income rating only by a modest $.71 (p < .05).

The average increase in the weekly income rating for mothers who were unemployed but looking for work was only slightly more than $6 more than that allotted to working mothers, and less than one half the $12.17 increase for unemployed fathers who were looking for work. For those vignettes where the mother was "more picky" about her employment, high sanctions were imposed. Vignettes where the mother was unemployed and not looking for work received $9.18 less than employed mothers (p < .05), while those who could not work because of a lack of transportation received $10.33 less (p < .01). Mothers who were unemployed because the only work available paid minimum wage, the average income rating was reduced more than $20 per week! (p < .001).

The two remaining family characteristics, the number of children in the vignette family, and that family's "cash flow", also had a strong effect on the overall income rating. The age of the youngest child, however, had virtually no effect on the overall rating. For each additional child in the vignette family, the income rating increased $12.26 per week (p < .001). For each dollar of savings the vignette family had on hand, the average weekly income rating was reduced by almost slightly less than $.01 (p < .10). In the GSS vignettes, family savings was either $0 (75 percent of the cases) or $1000 (25 percent). For each $1000 of family savings, therefore, the average weekly income rating was reduced by $3.77.

TABLE 3.5 Panel C: The GSS Study
Vignette Rating Regression

	B
Characteristics of Children (Continuous)	
Age of children	.18
Number of children	12.26***
Mothers marital status (married omitted)	
Mother divorced	-1.20
Mother never married	-3.18
Situation of father (employed omitted)	
Father disabled	26.01***
Father unemp, not looking	-7.13*
Father in prison	6.04#
Father unemp., Looking	12.17***
Mother's education (continuous)	
Child's mother's education	.71*
Mother's employment (working full time omitted)	
Mother works part time	.77
Mother looking for work	6.07#
Mother unemp, no child care	.25
Mother unemp, not looking	-9.19*
Mother unemp, no transport	-10.34**
Unemp, only min wage jobs	-20.52***
Father's marital status (blank omitted)	
father remarried	-.42
Financial prospects (difficult next 6 mo. omitted)	
Problems for next few years	4.81#
Problems continually in future	2.83
Parental help (parents help omitted)	
Parents cannot help	-.83
Parents could, but wont help	.52
Parents would, she wont ask	-4.70#
Family savings and income (continuous)	
Family's savings	-.004#
Family's income	.38***
(Constant)	149.39***

R Square	.145	
Adj R Square	.143	N = 974

= p<.10 * = p<.05 ** = p<.01 *** = p<.001 **** = p<.0001

In contrast to the effect of family savings, for each dollar of family weekly income the average weekly income rating given to the vignettes was *increased* by $.38 (p < .001), an increase, adjusted for the income amounts available to vignette families, of at least $19 per week (for families already receiving $50 in the vignette scenario).

The overall effect of the dimensions and levels used in the GSS study, allows us to better predict the income rating given to the vignettes. In the GSS vignette results, we are able to explain more than 14 percent of the variance in the amount of income awarded to the families by including only vignette characteristics in the equation. In addition, several dimensions stand out as especially important in determining the amount of income awarded to the vignette family. In particular, the dimensions dealing with the employment status of the vignette family mother and father, as well as the number of children in the family, and that family's weekly income, appear to be of primary importance.

COMPARABLE DATA, VARIABLE RESULTS

In the last section, two important points were discussed concerning the comparison of the Chicago, New York and GSS factorial surveys. First, as was expected, the issue of vignette design--particularly the number of dimensions used in the vignettes used--the complexity of the individual levels within dimensions, and the composition of the rating scale affected our ability to directly compare the studies. Second, generosity as portrayed in the vignette ratings differed as a result of these dimensions and levels. Dimensions and levels that varied within some studies (e.g. number of children and current levels of support) were absent within the third, thus restricting the comparison of the studies.

This section pares down each of the studies on several dimensions in order to more closely compare the impact of comparable dimensions and levels within each study vignette design. A perfect comparison of the three data sets is not possible: the Chicago study vignettes, because of the "multiple" stimuli in each level in a dimension, still must be used as the "least common denominator" and kept intact. As we discussed in the last chapter, the Chicago study contained the fewest number of dimensions (four) and each of these dimensions contained several components that were not varied between vignettes. In particular, each vignette in the Chicago study contained an unattached female vignette character, with two children (the youngest of which was 3 years old), with the family receiving $400 per month ($100 per week) in total outside support. The New York study and the GSS study each were reduced in size by selecting only those vignettes where the vignette character was an unattached female, with two children, and where the vignette family received only $100 per week in support (whether income or government assistance).

Vignette Specific Generosity.

Between study comparison of the amount of award given to the vignette scenario family is aided by the "paring down" studies so that there is a common "vignette space" for each study. In Table 3.6, the distribution of award amount for each of the studies is presented.[13] In this table, note that the Chicago vignette ratings have been adjusted to represent a WEEKLY award equivalent, rather than the monthly scale used in the actual study. Also, for ease of presentation, the New York study vignette ratings have been rounded to the nearest $10 increment.

As shown in Table 3.6, the distribution of weekly awards given to the vignettes portraying unattached women with two children for each of the studies is similar to those presented for the overall samples in the previous chapter. In particular, note that the average award for given to this sub-sample of vignette in the New York study is over $80 per week more than the weekly award given in Chicago. The average weekly award in the GSS vignettes is more than twice as high as the Chicago study, and more than $50 higher than the awards in the New York Study.

Note that, when compared to the average rating given to the overall sample of vignettes within the New York Study, vignettes depicting unattached women with two children averaged more than $40 per week in award. For the GSS vignettes, the average weekly award changed little when examining only the unattached women with two children vignettes.

TABLE 3.6 Panel A: The Chicago Study
Weekly Vignette Family Award
Unattached Women With 2 Children[14]

$ Award	%
$60.00	.2
$80.00	2.3
$90.00	3.6
$100.00	23.9
$110.00	22.5
$130.00	25.3
$140.00	8.2
$150.00	13.9

Mean   118.24   Median   113.00   N = 995

TABLE 3.6 Panel B: The New York City Study

$ Award	%	$ Award	%
0.00	7.9	210.00	1.3
10.00	.7	220.00	.8
20.00	.5	230.00	.3
30.00	.6	240.00	.1
40.00	.7	250.00	7.6
50.00	5.5	260.00	.2
60.00	.2	270.00	.6
70.00	.6	280.00	.7
80.00	1.6	290.00	.1
90.00	.8	300.00	10.6
100.00	10.4	310.00	.3
110.00	.7	320.00	.4
120.00	1.2	330.00	.6
130.00	1.4	340.00	.3
140.00	.4	350.00	7.0
150.00	10.7	360.00	.7
160.00	.4	370.00	1.3
170.00	.3	380.00	1.4
180.00	1.5	390.00	.4
190.00	.5	>400.00	8.0
200.00	10.8		

Mean	199.769	Median	200.000	Valid Cases	1084

TABLE 3.6 Panel C: The GSS Study
Weekly Vignette Family Award
For
Unattached Women with 2 Children

$ Award	%
$ 0	2.5
50	3.1
100	7.4
150	6.6
200	20.1
250	11.4
300	30.3
350	7.2
400	8.0
450	1.6
500	.9
550	.2
600	.6

MEAN 252.177 MEDIAN 250.000
VALID N = 2136

Vignette Characteristic Effects.

When examining the effects of the different components of these vignettes, we again see that specifically defined aspects of the vignettes affect respondents' generosity toward the vignette family. That is, even with each of the studies being pared down to represent only a select group of vignettes, when examining the results from the regression of vignette characteristics on the rating, some specific components of the New York and GSS studies still stand out. In Table 3.7, the results of these regressions are presented.[15]

As was expected, merely adjusting the Chicago study vignette ratings to represent weekly benefits had little impact on the effects of the vignette characteristics. As was also expected, by reducing the New York and GSS studies to vignettes with unattached women with two children, thus excluding some of the dimensions which were most effective in the full sample regressions (e.g number of children, marital status, employment status of spouse), the overall explanatory power as seen in the resulting R^2 in each regression is drastically reduced for these studies. However, several dimensions and levels within the New York and GSS studies remain important in respondents' generosity.

For the GSS vignettes, of primary importance to respondents' generosity, even for unattached women with two children, are those dimensions and levels dealing with employment status. In particular, for those vignettes where the vignette character was unemployed and not actively looking for work, respondents were punitive in their awarding of benefits compared to awards given to employed women. Punitive ratings ranged from a reduction of more than $24 for women who were simply "not looking for work," ($p < .001$) to reductions of more than $41 for women who do not work because of a lack of transportation ($p < .0001$). In vignettes where the estranged father of the child is unemployed and not looking, the weekly award is further reduced by over $20 compared to those vignettes where the estranged father was working ($p < .001$).

In the New York study, respondents again appeared to be more generous to those persons who were already receiving assistance. That is, even for those vignettes in which the number of children was held at two, respondents awarded 17 percent more for each dollar of government assistance already received ($p < .0001$). For each dollar of income the family received, awards were decreased by 31 percent (p < .0001). One unexpectedly important dimension in the New York study when examining this subset of the vignettes was the race of the vignette character. For those vignettes where the vignette character was white, the overall award was increased by more than $18 over those scenarios which did not mention the race of the character (p < .1). For vignettes where the person was black, the average rating increased by almost $26 per week (p < .01).

Note that in Panel B of table 3.7, those dimensions within the New York Study which most closely corresponded to those of the Chicago study had very little impact on the overall award. That is, for the Nutrition and Housing Conditions dimensions in the New York Study--levels within each correspond to some degree with the Nutrition, Housing, and Household Goods quality dimensions in the Chicago study--there were no characteristics which had an impact which was statistically significant at the .05 level. Only two levels (not being able to afford monthly movies in the Nutrition dimension and the too little heating level in the Housing conditions dimension) had effects that were significant at the p < .1 level, both of which escape an easily defendable explanation for such an impact. Again, the coefficients for these two dimensions were significant only at p < .1 level and thus were of little importance.

**TABLE 3.7 Panel A: The Chicago Study
Vignette Regression Analysis
For
Unattached Women with 2 Children**

	B
Neighborhood Quality	
Bad neighborhood	6.07***
Neighborhood ok	3.77**
Housing Quality	
Housing worst	3.57***
Household Goods Quality	
Worst household goods	9.78***
Ok household goods	4.09**
Nutrition Quality	
Worst nutrition	6.49***
Medium nutrition	3.61*
Health Care Quality	
Worst health care	2.37#
(Constant)	103.49***

R Square	.07330
Adjusted R Square	.06578

N = 995

TABLE 3.7 Panel B: The New York City Study
Vignette Regression Analysis
Unattached Women with 2 Children

	B
Race Of Vignette Character (blank text omitted)	
White vignette	18.12#
Black vignette	25.87**
Hispanic vignette	15.24
Education	
Education in vignette	-1.75
Marital Status (never married omitted)	
Deserted by spouse	13.20
Separated	4.28
Divorced	-2.39
Widowed	7.79
Employment Status (never worked omitted)	
Unemployed and not looking	-10.85
Unemployed and looking	-14.36
Employed persons	7.72
Nutrition (blank text omitted)	
2 Meals daily	-3.35
3 Meals daily with meat	-1.18
Can afford visiting rels	-16.12
Can't afford winter clothes	19.08
Can't afford a television	-16.12
Can't afford a telephone	-17.16
Can't afford monthly movies	-26.59#
Can't afford friends at dinner	-7.60
Can't afford restaurant	-9.64
Eat poorly & skip main meal	-7.22
No meat but 2 meals daily	-7.97

TABLE 3.7 Panel B: The New York City Study

	B
Housing Conditions (blank text omitted)	
All share the same bedroom	-15.96
Broken windows, poor plumbing	-6.46
Everyone has own bedroom	-7.38
Little heat in winter	-25.06#
Living room used for sleeping	-2.38
No heat or hot water, rats	6.95
One bedroom for all children	-2.55
One bed for all the kids	-6.10
Well maintained place	6.47
Expenditures	
Rent -amount spent on housing	.02
Cash Received	
Support payment from government	.17****
Earnings-take home wages of family	-.31****
(Constant)	208.88****

R Square	.07418
Adjusted R Square	.04418

F =   2.472
N =   1084

TABLE 3.7 Panel C: The GSS Study
Vignette Regression Analysis
Unattached Women with 2 Children

	B
Age of Youngest Child	
Age of youngest child	.37
Mother's Marital Status (divorced omitted)	
Mother never married	-1.56
Situation of Children's Father (employed omitted)	
Father disabled	3.73
Father unemp, not looking	-20.59***
Father unemp., Looking	-7.28
Father in prison	-10.64
Mother's Education	
Child's mother's education	.43
Mother's Employment Status (mother employed omitted)	
Mother works part time	2.37
Mother looking for work	-17.33*
Mother unemployed, no child care	-24.78***
Mother unemployed, not looking	-24.22***
Unemployed, only min wage jobs	-37.97****
Mother unemployed, no transport	-41.38****
Father's Marital Status (blank text omitted)	
Father remarried	1.26
Financial Prospects (problems next 6 months omitted)	
Problems continually in future	-1.90
Problems for next few years	6.77
Parental Help (Parents Help Omitted)	
Parents cannot help	-1.50
Parents could, but won't help	4.28
Parents would, she won't ask	-4.34
Family Savings and Income	
Family savings	.01
Total family income	-1.64*
(Constant)	287.21****

R Square   .03348
Adjusted R Square   .02347   N = 2049

COMPARING THE STUDIES

In this chapter we have examined the design and basic results of three studies conducted to measure attitudes and beliefs about the poor. In each of the studies, a relatively recent development in social science research, the factorial survey, was employed to examine the extent to which various situational characteristics confronting low income families affect the degree of external support that family deserves. Each of these studies used a different factorial design and each obtained somewhat different results.

Design Characteristics.

Of the three factorial surveys, the one design that stood out as quite different in approach was the Chicago study. In Chicago, Love and Frankfather restricted the conditions portrayed in the vignettes to those most "normally" faced by welfare recipients they had previously studied. Only five dimensions were employed in the Chicago study, each containing a maximum of three levels. In addition, their design employed broadly defined dimensions and levels, with each level of a dimension containing several pieces of information, each of which addressed a different aspect of that condition. Thus when stating that a person had the "worst" nutrition level, both quantity and quality of the diet are addressed. Levels in other dimensions are similarly complex. Also, in each of the Chicago study vignette, the family size and income are constant throughout the packet, with only the vignette character's name changing.

The New York and General Social Survey vignette designs, however, allow for all combinations available in a full factorial designs. These studies included 18 and 11 dimensions respectively, with the number of levels in any one dimensions ranging from two (family savings in the GSS study) to 17 or more (the Occupation and government support dimensions in the New York Study). Each dimension in these studies contains specific information about only one aspect of the vignette family's condition, thus allowing each piece of information to be examined independently. Of particular importance here is the use of a variable number of children throughout the vignettes, and including changes in income and other government support.

In addition, the Chicago study provided three rating scales for each vignette. The Hardship and Adequacy ratings in the Chicago study examined extent to which respondents had sympathy, while the third scale asked respondents to state what the vignette family deserved in monthly AFDC support. The New York and GSS study vignettes included only one rating scale per vignette. In New York, respondents were asked to determine the level of public assistance each vignette family deserved, while the GSS vignette rating asked for the weekly income figure that respondents felt the vignette family should get.

Finally, in both the Chicago and the New York studies, a less than optimal sampling design was used in selecting respondents. For the Chicago study, the sample was drawn by randomly selecting one person from each voting precinct within the City of Chicago. In New York, a quota sampling design was utilized, selecting for equal number of respondents according race, income, age and gender. For the General Social Survey, however, a national probability sample of respondents was collected. With the New York and Chicago studies, generalization of findings, to the extent that such generalization could be done, was possible only to the respective cities. With the GSS study, we are able to extrapolate to the nation as a whole.

Different and Similar Findings.

When comparing the findings of the three studies, it appears that in each study some dimensions and levels have a stronger effect on the responses to the ratings than others, yet the degree of impact is not as straightforward as might be expected. In the Chicago study, we find that *every* dimension has a strong and statistically significant effect on the amount of money the poor family deserves. Yet despite the strong net effects of each of these dimensions, we are able to explain only a small portion of the variance in the rating scale by using the vignette characteristics. It appears that the "strength" of each of the dimensions is therefore less useful for understanding generosity than at first appears. The overall inability of the dimensions and levels to account for changes in the rating, coupled with the complexity of the components of individual levels within the dimensions, makes solid conclusions somewhat difficult to address.

In the New York and GSS studies, with dimensions that are much more specific, the independent effects of the different levels of the dimensions are more straight-forward. In addition, the inclusion of dimensions and levels, in particular the use of family income and number of children, as variable dimensions rather than constants greatly enhanced our ability to examine the effect these conditions have on respondents' judgments of need. In both the New York and GSS studies, the inclusion of the income and number of children variables proved to be essential, as these variables ranked among the strongest.

Results from the New York study, however, also indicate that some limits on the size and content of the vignettes may also be needed. Several dimensions in that study appeared to be inconsequential to the overall rating, and in several other dimensions many of the levels proved insignificant. Similarly, the GSS results warrant a review of the decision for inclusion of some dimensions, and perhaps point to the inclusion of others.

In the following chapters, the focus will be placed on the General Social Survey. In these chapters, individual respondent characteristics and vignette characteristics will be used to examine the levels of generosity of the American public, and the extent to which the information obtained from the GSS can be used to discuss national priorities and national policy.

NOTES

1. For a complete discussion of the data collection procedures, see Lois Thessien Love, *The Extent of Public Obligation: Minimally Acceptable Living Conditions as Perceived by Chicago Area Voters*, Unpublished Dissertation, University of Chicago, 1986.

2. For a complete discussion of these interviews, see Frankfather, *Preliminary Report: Life Circumstances of AFDC Recipients*, unpublished report, University of Chicago.

3. For full details of the New York Study, See Joseph Pereira, 1986. *Who Should Be Supported: New Yorkers Normative Views of Welfare Entitlement.* Unpublished Dissertation, University of Massachusetts, Amherst.

4. Although there were 18 different dimensions included in the vignette design, no single vignette included every dimension. Various restrictions on combinations of levels and dimensions, for example in the work status dimensions, were used in the design, thus reducing the total number of dimensions allowed in each vignette.

5. Half way through the data collection, after receiving indication that some respondents felt the $400 limit was too restrictive, Pereira and Rossi instructed the interviewers to allow respondents to write in amounts more than $400 that the respondent felt justified.

6. The GSS has actually been conducted each year since 1972, with the exception of 1979 and 1981. It has been based on a National Probability Sample since 1975. For most years, supplemental sections of the survey are added in order to focus on particular methodological or substantive issues. For example, the 1985 GSS included a "network analysis" supplement.

7. The Chicago Study scale had both dollar amounts and a single digit numeric scale.

8. Represents Dollar amount after conversion of from 9 point scale.

9. "Net Benefits" represents the total amount of money allotted to the vignette family, after the current income and/or government assistance received by the vignette family has been subtracted from the vignette award.

10. For purposes of comparing the General Social Survey Vignettes with those of the other two studies, only the vignettes depicting young families are included in this table.

11. In order to more accurately discuss the comparisons between the studies, "Benefits" in the Chicago study refer to the rating scale which has been adjusted to represent dollars, rather than the 9 point scale used in the original questionnaire.

12. The New York Study vignettes contained several dimensions that will not be addressed in this chapter. Specifically, occupation status and reasons for being out of work (unemployed and looking, unemployed and not looking, and never worked) are omitted from this discussion in order to allow the focus to be placed on the comparison of the 3 studies. For a full discussion of the new York Study, see Rossi and Pereira. (1986).

13. For purposes of comparing levels of awards between the studies, the Living Conditions rating and the Degree of Hardship rating from the Chicago study are not presented.

14. For purposes of comparison, the Chicago Study awards were converted to represent **weekly** awards, rather than monthly. To this end, awards were divided by 4. The Mean award was calculated only for ratings after transformation to dollars.

15. Again, note that the New York Study has been adjusted to represent WEEKLY benefit awards.

CHAPTER 4

CHARACTERISTICS OF GENEROSITY: THE NATIONAL CASE

INTRODUCTION.

In the last chapter we examined the overall levels of generosity as found in three separate studies. Differences in levels of generosity, and the effect of the characteristics of each of the factorial survey designs used in those studies on generosity, were compared across the three studies in order to assess the impact of vignette size and composition of the studies. In this chapter, we will focus on the substantive issues of generosity toward the poor, and on the variations in generosity found among different segments of the general population. To this end, this chapter will focus on the results of the 1986 General Social Survey, and accompanying factorial survey component.

As was stated in the last chapter, the General Social Survey (GSS) is an annual, national sample survey conducted by the National Opinion Research Center at the University of Chicago. The 1986 GSS represents the first national sample survey to utilize the Factorial Survey methodology. In addition, the GSS offers a wide range of behavioral, attitudinal and demographic information on respondents. With the combination of having a national sample, and a wide variety of respondent characteristics, a more thorough examination of respondents' perspectives on the poor and the levels of generosity displayed toward low income individuals can be made.

EXAMINING VARIATIONS IN GENEROSITY

As we discussed in the last chapter, each respondent in the 1986 GSS received seven vignettes, each depicting a young female headed family living below, or near the poverty line. For each of these vignettes, respondents were asked to indicate what that family's weekly income **should** be, including money the family may already be earning and any government assistance payments that the respondent felt the vignette family deserved. In this chapter, this "overall weekly income" given to the vignette families will be referred to as "generosity".

In this context, therefore, generosity refers primarily to overall level of income awarded to vignette families rather than an indication of respondent personal integrity. That is, the level of generosity given by various sub-groups of the population is not intended to be an indication of the level of "moral" responsibility or integrity portrayed by those groups. Also, given that respondents could easily have indicated that the vignette families deserved no assistance, any award could therefore be considered generous. Throughout this chapter, therefore, generosity refers to the actual award (or average award) given to the vignette family.

In the previous chapter we found that the weekly income awarded to the vignette families was strongly affected by the conditions portrayed in the vignette scenario. This offered strong support for anticipating that conditions and characteristics of respondents also will affect levels of generosity. The question addressed here, therefore, is whether the respondents, independently of what the vignette scenario portrays, are predisposed toward particular levels of generosity.

However, some concerns surface when our analysis changes from multivariate examination of vignette characteristics to the bivariate examination of individual, or aggregate, level characteristics. With each respondent having evaluated seven vignettes[1], the number of respondent level observations is inflated for the vignette level analysis. That is, the total N represents one "respondent record" for each vignette evaluated. With this inflated N, there is some concern with a biasing of significance tests. In particular, the inflated N drives the significance levels up somewhat artificially, inhibiting the ability to rely on tests of significance.

On the other hand, reducing the analysis to the aggregate, or individual level, and focusing the analysis on the average evaluation given by respondents over the total number of vignette scenarios evaluated, other concerns arise. In particular, there is a concern with the effect outlier vignettes may have on the respondent's average. That is, with only seven vignettes per respondent, out of a possible 1.3 million (approximate) vignettes, the "average" rating could be affected by the vignette content more strongly than if respondents received a much larger number of vignettes (say 30). If, for example, a respondent's packet included only vignettes in which the mother's work status indicated that they were not working because of only minimum wage jobs, no transportation, or inadequate daycare--levels of work status that were found to greatly reduce the weekly income award--the respondent's predisposed level of generosity could be seen as only partially driving the individual vignette scenario evaluation.

Another concern with using the respondent's average vignette award is that any impact on the respondents judgement created by the vignette dimensions and levels is relegated to unexplained error within the equation--by collapsing the responses to vignettes into the mean award, the independent effects of the dimensions and level can not be assessed. Although independence of effect can be insured when examining the vignette dimensions and levels, such assurances cannot be maintained at the respondent aggregate level.

In order to address both the concerns associated with each of these analysis levels, as well as to take advantage of the benefits each level offers, both individual (respondent) level and vignette level analysis will be examined. Analysis of variance techniques will be used to analyze individual mean level data, insuring our ability to analyze variations in generosity between subgroups of respondents and to examine the overall effect of respondent characteristics. In addition, by adding respondent characteristics to the vignette level analysis conducted in the last chapter, multiple regression techniques will be used to determine the independent effects of respondent characteristics.

VARIATION IN RESPONDENT CHARACTERISTICS

As stated above, using the respondent average vignette award allows for the examination of more general patterns of generosity. Overall differences in levels of generosity, for example, among racial or religious group can thus be examined by using the mean respondent vignette award. This distribution of average respondent level of generosity, like the distribution of income awards given to the various vignettes, reveals the variation among the respondents predispositions.

Indeed, an examination of the distribution of average vignette rating given by respondents illustrates the extent of the variation between respondents.

In table 4.1, the distribution of the average vignette award is presented.[2] As can be seen in Table 4.1, the ground mean of vignette income awards is slightly more than $256 per week, with a median "average" income award of $250 per week. In addition, fewer than 20 percent of the respondents gave an average income award of less than $200 per week, with more than 92 percent of all respondents awarding an average weekly income award of more than $150. Five percent of the respondents awarded an average of $400 or more per week--amounts that exceeded the "average U.S. family weekly income" of $400 as presented on the rating scale of each vignette given to respondents.

Now several important points can be taken from this table. First, as shown in the last chapter and further confirmed here the large number of vignette awards above the $200 level seems to indicate that there is a basic "floor" below which few of the vignette families should be allowed to fall. Second, the implications of this floor are most important for the interpretation of these result when compared with the actual conditions of poor families: in fact, the floor at which most of these vignette families were protected is more than twice the average weekly AFDC award given in the United States (see: *Statistical Abstracts of the United States*, 1989, p. 367).

That is, although not all vignette families are equally rated as to their needed income, almost 90 percent of all of the respondents averaged giving the fictitious vignette families almost twice the average U.S. weekly AFDC award of approximately $85.

TABLE 4.1

Average Weekly Income Award to Vignette Families

Avg $ Award	%	Avg $ Award	%
.00	.1	280.00	3.6
10.00	.1	290.00	3.4
20.00	.1	300.00	5.5
30.00	.2	310.00	2.3
40.00	.1	320.00	4.8
50.00	.3	330.00	1.5
60.00	.3	340.00	1.0
70.00	.6	350.00	3.0
80.00	.4	360.00	.7
90.00	.3	370.00	2.2
100.00	.7	380.00	.7
110.00	.3	390.00	.5
120.00	1.4	400.00	1.5
130.00	.5	410.00	.7
140.00	1.5	420.00	.6
150.00	2.0	430.00	.1
160.00	2.0	440.00	.2
170.00	3.8	450.00	.8
180.00	2.0	460.00	.2
190.00	3.0	470.00	.1
200.00	5.9	480.00	.1
210.00	3.8	490.00	.1
220.00	9.9	500.00	.2
230.00	3.8	510.00	.1
240.00	4.5	540.00	.1
250.00	8.6	590.00	.1
260.00	3.9	600.00	.1
270.00	5.7		

Mean   256.18   Median 250.0
Valid Cases 1380

Finally, although there is a floor that seems to demarcate a level below which most of the vignette families should not fall, and despite the bunching of responses around the $200--$300 range, we still find significant variation within the distribution of respondents' average awards. That is, although the makeup of the individual vignette scenario and the dimensions and levels within the vignettes do affect how respondents perceived the vignette families' need, by examining the average award given by respondents we see there is still a significant amount of variation that can be addressed through examining subgroups of the respondent population.

Thus, in addition to the effects that various components of the vignette scenario have on the dollar amount being awarded, characteristics of the respondents also have an impact upon levels of generosity. In particular, demographic characteristics such as the race, sex, education, income and geographical location, and political orientation characteristics such as political party identification and the liberal-conservative scale self identification ratings may offer some insight into the underlying structure of generosity toward these vignettes.

In order to interpret properly this distribution in average income award, we will focus on two primary influences we believe to affect such generosity. These influences include the presence of empathy/sympathy (increased respondent support for the vignette families precipitated by similar personal demographic or experiential characteristics which place one at risk of the effects of poverty) and "ideological" factors (the general political ideology, and attitudinal positions toward low income persons, and the effect of poverty on individuals, held by the various subgroups of respondents). For the remainder of this chapter, those influences associated with the respondents' being at risk, or the empathy/sympathy for the plight of the vignette family, will be examined.

RESPONDENT EMPATHY/SYMPATHY: A SENSE OF RISK

The effects of poverty are not only felt by those suffering from insufficient resources, but also by people who are acquainted with poverty through past experience or sympathy, as well as those who fit into the poverty prone subgroups of the population. A person does not need be poor to recognize the plight of the poor. Similarly, one's recognition of poverty conditions does not necessarily imply sympathy or empathy, nor do such feelings necessarily lead to increased levels of generosity toward the poverty stricken. Indeed, the "Eboneezer Scrooge" caricature acknowledged the existence of the poor, but showed little compassion, if any.

What is of interest here, therefore, is to examine the relationship between the characteristics of respondents with the levels of generosity toward the vignette characters. Do people who fit similar life situations as portrayed in the vignettes exhibit higher levels of generosity than those who do not? To what extent, that is, do respondents who would intuitively be considered sympathetic or empathetic to the plight of the disadvantaged show higher levels of generosity than those who do not fit the sympathetic design. Of primary interest here are the basic respondent demographic characteristics not included in the vignette design that are believed to influence levels of generosity (respondent sex, race, age, etc.), as well as respondent characteristics that are similar to vignette family characteristics, including socio-economic characteristics (respondent income, work status, education, etc.), and characteristics of the respondent's residential situation (number and age of children, marital status, experience with public assistance, etc).

Empathy and Generosity: Non-vignette Characteristics.

Considerations of time, respondent fatigue, and theoretical and programmatic issues limited the scope of the vignettes used in the GSS vignettes. Because of these design issues, some dimensions, which would otherwise be considered a strong indicator of generosity, had to be omitted. In particular, demographic characteristics such as the race, sex, and age of the vignette characters were not included in the design of the vignettes.

However, the omission of these dimensions from the actual design of the vignettes does not prohibit the "implied" effect various levels of these dimensions could have on respondent generosity. Indeed, within the framework of the empathy/sympathy effect on generosity, the influences such dimensions could have on the levels of generosity can be discussed in light of the respondents characteristics. This is not to say that these dimensions were completely absent from the vignette design. By design, all of the vignettes discussed either households female headed or intact family households--thus some comparison can be made between male and female vignette characters. Also, the age of the vignette mother is implied in the scenario--the age of the child rules out, for the most part, the possibility of the age of the vignette mother being above the mid to late 30's. In addition, a separate set of vignettes was presented to each respondent depicting old (65 and 75 years of age), widowed women[3], thus some comparison can be made.

Other characteristics seen by some researchers as important when examining attitudes toward the poor, most notably the race of the poor family and the physical condition of the family head (in the case of female headed households), are, however, not included in the vignette design. Indeed, deliberations on the design of the vignettes (in conjunction with findings in the pretest as reported in Pereira, 1988), specifically ruled out inclusion of race as a dimension in the vignettes. In addition, while physical condition of the father of the children in the vignette scenario does include a reference to "disabled," no such dimension is included for the vignette family mother. Finally, issues concerning the quality of life of the vignette family, including housing quality and type, and subjective concerns of the relative condition of the family, also were omitted from the GSS vignettes. For these vignettes' characteristics, the impact on level of generosity can be examined through respondent characteristics.

Non-Matched Characteristics.

In order to examine fully the effect that empathy or sympathy has on a respondent's level of generosity, all relevant dimensions to be examined would have to be contained in the makeup of the vignette as well as the makeup of the respondents. As we have seen, however, not all of what are believed to be relevant respondent characteristics were included in the vignette design. Yet, despite the absence of some respondent characteristics, hypotheses that increased levels of generosity exhibited toward the vignette scenarios may be generated from empathetic or sympathetic concerns--the respondent either has experienced the hardships of poverty or belongs to one or more subgroups of the population that experience such hardships in larger than expected proportion--can still be examined.

Much of the recent literature on poverty has focused on the prevalence of poverty among families, especially female headed families with young children. Indeed, much of the focus seems to be on the effect poverty has on women and their families. Within this focus, therefore, empathy/sympathy influences would be expected to show that women respondents display higher levels of generosity exhibited toward the vignette families than do men. Specifically, it was anticipated that women would be significantly more generous than men toward the vignette characters, particularly since a majority of the vignettes centered on currently unattached women with children.

However, as can be seen in Figure 4.1, only small differences in levels of generosity were found between male and female respondents. In addition, this small difference is not statistically significant (at $p < .10$). For women respondents, the average award is slightly more than $258 per week, while for male respondents the average weekly award is $253. Although we believed women, an increased number of whom are more vulnerable to poverty, would show much higher levels of generosity because of the empathy factor, women averaged only about $20 more per month in income awards to the vignettes than males.

In contrast to the small differences found when comparing the levels of generosity displayed by female and male respondents, variations in generosity by different racial groups proved quite strong. Again, most available statistics show that blacks and, increasingly, hispanics are highly over represented in the poverty ranks, with more than 30 percent of all blacks and over 28 percent of hispanics earning incomes below the poverty line (*Statistical Abstracts of the United States*, 1989.p 452).

Figure 4.1
Generosity Level by Sex of Respondent

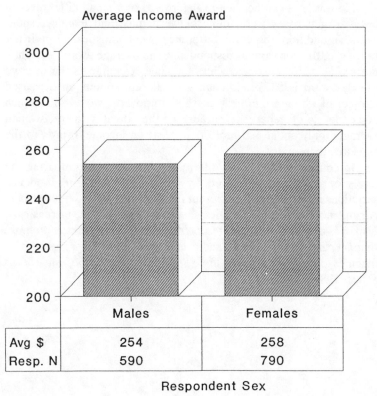

Average Income Award

	Males	Females
Avg $	254	258
Resp. N	590	790

Respondent Sex

▨ Avg $

Differences not significant

Thus it was expected that the levels of generosity displayed by non-whites would be significantly greater than the average levels of generosity for whites. Indeed, as can be seen in Figure 4.2, the average award given by blacks is more than $44 per week higher than the average award given by whites. In addition, those respondents of "other races" (which are not specifically identified in the GSS) average $30 and more in awards than whites (p < .0001). Combining these other races with blacks results in average income ratings of more than $292 per week, $32 higher than awards given by white respondents. These differences between the average income awards of white respondents and non-whites, particularly in light of the large proportion of the minority population in the U.S. that lives below the poverty line, were somewhat expected. Although the actual monetary difference in awards given by male and female respondents is not very large (approximately $20 per month), the difference between whites and nonwhites is quite large--averaging almost $170 per month more for awards given by non-whites.

In addition to the differences found when examining the race of the respondent, we can also easily examine the interaction between race and sex. Indeed, as we find in Figure 4.2A, what small amount of gender difference that does exist is an interaction between the race and sex of the respondents. In Figure 4.2A we find that there is virtually no difference between the average award given by white males and white females; rather, the dramatic differences are between black females and whites (+ $52), and black males and whites (+ $26). In addition, we also find and average award difference of $26 between black males and black females, with the vignette awards given by black females averaging more than $302 per week. Thus those most affected by the conditions of poverty, in particular non-white women, display the most empathy/sympathy, and are by far the most generous toward the vignette families.

Figure 4.2
Generosity Level by Respondent Race

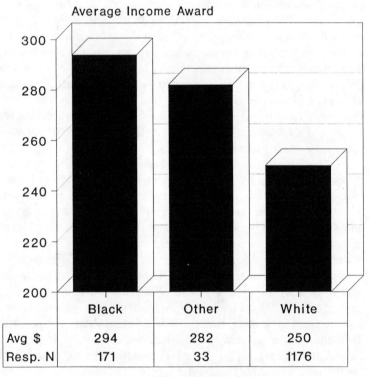

Average Income Award

Respondent Race	Black	Other	White
Avg $	294	282	250
Resp. N	171	33	1176

Respondent Race

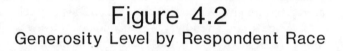 Avg $

Differences sig. p <.001

Figure 4.2a
Generosity Level Race-Sex Comparison

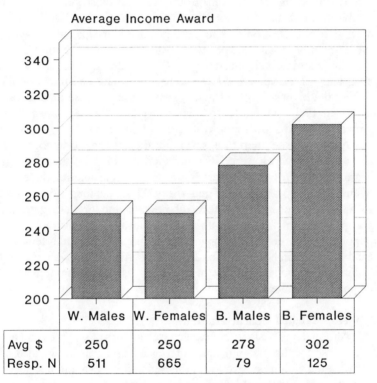

Average Income Award

	W. Males	W. Females	B. Males	B. Females
Avg $	250	250	278	302
Resp. N	511	665	79	125

Respondent Characteristics

▨ Avg $

Differences sig. p <.001

In addition to differences by race and sex, significant differences were found for the various age cohorts. In Figure 4.3, the distribution of award by age is presented. When examining the average award by age category, we find that those respondents whose cohort reached adulthood during the 1970s--the 35 to 44 year old cohort--are the least generous, with the average weekly award of $245. The youngest cohort--the 18 to 24 year old group--was the most generous, with weekly awards averaging more than $270 per week. The elderly, those 65 and over, represented the next generous groups, with awards averaging more than $262 per week. Again, although the differences are only marginally significant ($p < .05$), we find that those persons most likely to be vulnerable to poverty, the young and the very old, display the highest levels of generosity. Those who are most estab-lished in their careers, respondents aged 35 to 64, appear less sympathetic and show the lowest levels of generosity.[4]

As we can see, therefore, several basic respondent demographic characteristics which were NOT included within the vignette design characteristics, prove to be very important when examining the effect of empathy factors on level of generosity. Those persons MOST likely to have experienced the effects of poverty and/or belong to the groups that are prevalent within the disadvantaged portion of the population (particularly young respondents, blacks, and females) exhibit much higher levels of generosity than those who are not traditionally thought of as in need of assistance--middle aged respondents, whites, and males.

Vignette-Matched Characteristics.

Although the basic respondent characteristics of sex, race and age did prove to show significant differences in levels of generosity between the various subgroups of the population, it should not neces-sarily be assumed that the quality of the vignette design suffered form their omission. Rather, by combining these characteristics that were omitted from the design (yet are seen as related to poverty concerns) with those characteristics included in the vignette design, we are able to develop fully the empathy/sympathy factor argument.

Figure 4.3
Generosity Level by Respondent Age

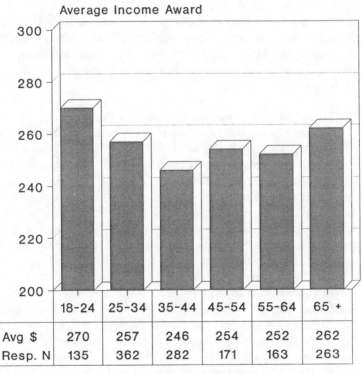

Average Income Award

	18-24	25-34	35-44	45-54	55-64	65 +
Avg $	270	257	246	254	252	262
Resp. N	135	362	282	171	163	263

Respondent Age

Avg $

Differences sig. p <.05

Not all of the vignette characteristics can, however, be directly matched with similar respondent characteristics, although more indirect measures will be examined. Those items include the financial prospects facing the family over the next few years, and the extent of parental assistance received. However, a majority of the dimensions used in the vignette construction can be closely matched to respondents. These include the number and age of the children in the household, marital status, education level and income level. In addition, more indirectly implied characteristics, particularly whether the respondent has ever received welfare, if the respondent has ever been unemployed or has ever been divorced (as opposed to currently being so) and other items indicating recent physical or financial hardships.

Similarity in Family Type: Age/Number of Children.

As was discussed in the last chapter, when we examined the effects of vignette family characteristics on levels of generosity, as the number of children in the scenario increased, the amount of the vignette award increased dramatically (p < .000). When the age of the youngest child in the vignette family was examined, however, there was little increase in the award given. From this, it would be assumed that, within the empathy/sympathy framework, we would expect to find that those with increasing numbers of children would show increasing levels of generosity.

As can be seen in Figure 4.4, however, when we examine the average award given to the vignettes, by the number of children the respondent has, we find that those who are most generous are, in fact, those with NO children at all. For those respondents who do not have children, the average income awarded to the vignette families is more than $265 per week -$10 more per week than the amount awarded by those with one child, and over $15 per week more than was awarded by those with two children. Only small differences can be found when comparing the average income award for persons with three or more children. Indeed, the primary difference is between those with no children and those with one or more children.

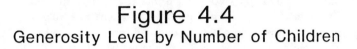

Figure 4.4
Generosity Level by Number of Children

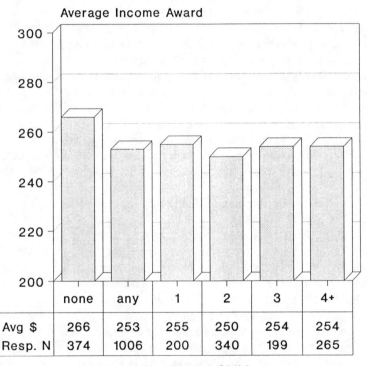

Average Income Award

	none	any	1	2	3	4+
Avg $	266	253	255	250	254	254
Resp. N	374	1006	200	340	199	265

Number of Children

☐ Avg $

None-Any differences sig. p <.01
Number of Children sig. p <.10

When examining levels of generosity, we find the average income awarded by childless respondents ($265.52) is almost $13 higher than those respondents who are parents ($252.71, difference = p .01). However, when we examine the differences in levels of generosity given by respondents with young children, compared to those with older children, significant difference is evident.

Although the GSS survey instrument does not specify age of the youngest child, there are items that address the presence of young children of various age groups. Of particular interest here is the item ascertaining whether the respondent has a child under the age of 6 living in the household. Within the vignette design, 2/3 of the levels dealing with child age were below 6 years (6 months of age and 4 years). And, as was discussed in the previous chapter, no significant differences were found between the various ages of the vignette family children. Yet, intuitively one would expect respondents with young children to be somewhat more generous. As parents of young children, and, for the most part, young adults, they would be expected to feel the brunt of the financial responsibilities associated with the care of young children.

Indeed, as can be seen in Figure 4.5, although those with young children do not exhibit levels as high as those with no children, they award significantly higher income awards than those who have children who are all over the age of six (p < .01). Again, however, we find that those with NO children are still the most generous of the subgroups being examined. Those persons who do have children, who are all over the age of six, are the least generous.

At first glance, the increased levels of generosity found for those without children at all appears somewhat misplaced, because it could be easily assumed that those persons without children would be, by virtue of not having the additional responsibility of caring for a young child, less inclined to exhibit high levels of generosity. As we stated above, however, the age of the respondent was found to be an additional empathy influence on level of generosity. The increased generosity displayed here, we believe, represents those young persons.

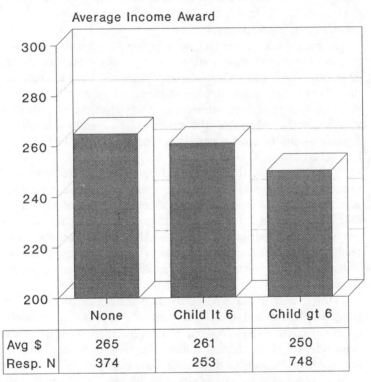

Figure 4.5
Generosity Level by Age of Children

Average Income Award

	None	Child lt 6	Child gt 6
Avg $	265	261	250
Resp. N	374	253	748

Presence/Age of Children

Avg $

Differences sig. p <.01

Respondent Marital Status.

The levels of generosity stemming from the sympathy influence can also be addressed by examining the income award differences by marital status. We would expect those who are not secure in their relationship to be more sympathetic than attached respondents. Indeed, the differences between married and non-married respondents appears to indicate the effect of such empathy/sympathy factors does exist. In Figure 4.6, the average income award is presented by marital status of respondent.

In Figure 4.6, we see that those people who have never married and those who are separated, but not yet divorced, are the most generous. These groups average approximately $20 per week more than those respondents who are widowed, and almost $25 per week more than those who are married. (p < .0001). Again note that those who are most vulnerable--the never married and those who are separated--are the most generous, while those in stable situations are less generous.

Note, however, that divorced respondents award virtually the same (only $3 more) in weekly income as married respondents, whereas those who are separated are the most generous of all groups. One possible explanation for this difference is that separated persons are currently experiencing some of the hurdles as the vignette families (and poor families in general)--recent financial hardships associated with the separation, residential instability, etc--and thus are far more likely to feel sympathy for the vignette family.

Differences in the generosity levels, by marital status, when comparing male and female respondents appears to support the sympathy factor as well. As can be seen in Figure 4.6a, the levels of generosity for those marital status categories that were considered less stable are somewhat different for male and female respondents. That is, those respondents who are in the more vulnerable position exhibit higher levels of generosity than the less vulnerable.

Figure 4.6
Generosity Level by Marital Status

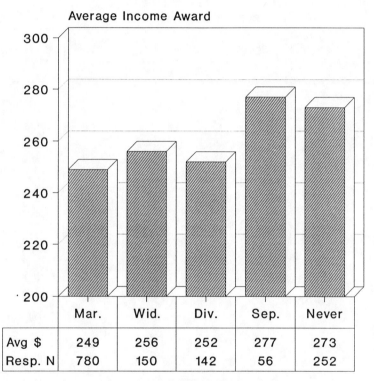

Average Income Award

	Mar.	Wid.	Div.	Sep.	Never
Avg $	249	256	252	277	273
Resp. N	780	150	142	56	252

Marital Status

▨ Avg $

Differences sig. p <.001

Figure 4.6a
Generosity for Gender-Marital Status

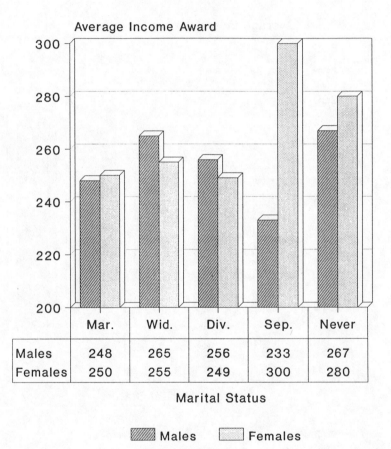

Average Income Award

	Mar.	Wid.	Div.	Sep.	Never
Males	248	265	256	233	267
Females	250	255	249	300	280

Marital Status

◆ Males □ Females

Differences sig. p <.001

This can be seen most dramatically in the differences between males and females who are separated, where women average more than $70 more per week in award than males who are separated. Women who have never been married are also more generous than their male counterparts, averaging more than $413 per week more in income award than never married males.

Strong differences also can be seen, however, when we examine those marital situations in which the male may be most vulnerable. Specifically, as can be seen in Figure 4.6a, widowed and divorced males show higher levels of generosity than similarly situated females, with divorced males awarding more than $10 per week more in awards than divorced females. Virtually no differences in levels of generosity are found between males and females who are married, the situation considered to be the most stable.[5]

Respondent Education.

The role that respondent education level plays within the empathy/sympathy framework is not as easily to tease out as it can be when examining other characteristics (e.g. gender, race, etc). Two somewhat contradictory perspectives could be presented concerning the effect of education. Within the sympathy discussion we would have expected those persons with lower levels of education to be more generous than higher education levels by virtue of their lower employment levels, employment status and levels of income. On the other hand, increased education levels often are cited as important indicators of social responsibility.

However, examining the differences in levels of generosity toward the vignette families the level of education has virtually no effect. In fact, with only one group--those with only a high school diploma--do we see ANY variation from the other education levels. As can be seen in Figure 4.7, the only fluctuations in the levels of generosity were found in those with only a high school diploma, where the average award was $251 per week. The remaining education levels averaged awards of approximately $258 per week. These differences were significant only at the $p < .05$ level.

Figure 4.7
Generosity Level by Education Level

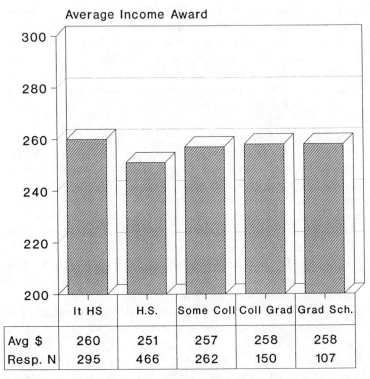

	It HS	H.S.	Some Coll	Coll Grad	Grad Sch.
Avg $	260	251	257	258	258
Resp. N	295	466	262	150	107

Education Level

▨ Avg $

Differences sig. p ‹.05

Thus, as we can see, the differences in generosity shown between various education levels do not significantly add to our empathy-/sympathy framework. No strong effect exhibited by respondent education level can be seen when examining the levels of generosity toward the vignette families. Similarly, only slight differences can be seen when examining the levels of generosity toward the vignette family mother, when examining her education level.

Respondent Work Status.
Sympathy-related increases in levels of generosity are also evident when examining the work status of respondents. Those respondents who are unemployed or unable to work and those who are retired would, within the empathy/sympathy framework, be expected to be more generous than those who are in more stable situations--particularly the employed, "homemakers" and students. In figure 4.8 the average income award is presented for the levels of respondent work status.

As can be seen in Figure 4.8, those who are unemployed[6] and those who have retired are by far the most generous, averaging over $20 more per week than full-time employed respondents, those keeping house and those in school (p < .000). Although few in number, respondents in school are the least generous in weekly income award, a contrast to what was expected. Respondents who are in school, traditionally the youngest cohort, in fact average more than $20 less in weekly award than the overall young cohort, and $25 less than those who are young and **not** students.

In addition to variations in generosity by the respondents' work status, the overall effect of household work status also represents an important consideration when examining the effects of the empathy/sympathy factors. Particularly for those persons who married, the presence of a spouse who works would be expected to lessen the empathetic effects--particularly for those dual income producing couples. Similarly, it would be expected that those persons from families where BOTH persons are unemployed (or underemployed), the level of generosity toward the vignette families would increase.

Figure 4.8
Generosity Level by Work Status

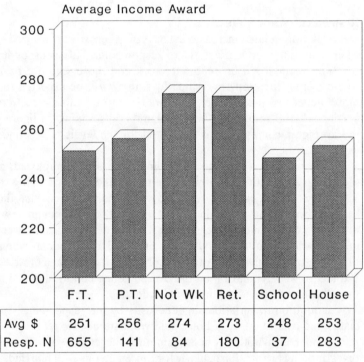

Average Income Award

	F.T.	P.T.	Not Wk	Ret.	School	House
Avg $	251	256	274	273	248	253
Resp. N	655	141	84	180	37	283

Work Status

■ Avg $

Differences sig. p <.001
Not Wk includes unemp, laid off, other

Being out of work or retired also are indicators of decreased earning power and household income. And, as was expected, those whose income is low--and thus represent a more sympathetic group-- also are the most generous toward the vignette families. In figure 4.9, the average award rating is presented for respondent household income. In figure 4.9, we find that the higher the persons household income, the less generous she/he tends to be, while those who are the least well-off (i.e. incomes of less than $15,000) are the most generous (p < .000). Note that, in presenting respondent household income in categories as we have here, there is a distinct trend for the average income award levels to decrease as income increase. However, there are also fluctuations in this trend, particularly noticeable in the relatively low award levels for the 15--20,000 income group.

VOICES OF EXPERIENCE.

As we have seen in the previous discussion, there appears to be a significant amount of support for the empathy/sympathy influence of respondent characteristics on level of generosity. Those respon- dents most likely to be in subgroups of the population prone to suffering the effects of poverty show higher levels of generosity than those not falling into those subgroups. Non-whites, particularly non- white women, the very old, and the very young adults, families with very young children, and those facing hardships associated with unemployment and lower income all show increased levels of generosity.

In addition to the effects associated with these personal traits, we also find increased levels of generosity being shown by those who directly **experienced** some of the hardships. In particular, respondents who have received public assistance, and those living in areas most affected by the presence of poverty--large metropolitan area residents and those living in financially burdened regions of the country--would be expected to show higher levels of generosity by virtue of having higher levels of empathy/sympathy for the vignette family.

Figure 4.9
Generosity Level by Income

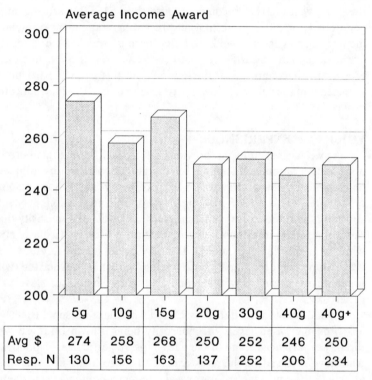

	5g	10g	15g	20g	30g	40g	40g+
Avg $	274	258	268	250	252	246	250
Resp. N	130	156	163	137	252	206	234

Income Level

☐ Avg $

Differences sig. p <.01

Assistance Recipients.

Having the direct experience of actually receiving government assistance, or welfare, can be considered to be an important influence on the level of generosity shown toward the welfare families. It could be asked, who better to have a grasp on the financial needs facing welfare recipients than a past, or current, recipient of such assistance? In the 1986 GSS survey, respondents were asked whether "you personally ever received income from Aid to Families with Dependent Children, General Assistance, Supplemental Security Income, or Food Stamps?" In all, of those persons answering the question, slightly more than 19 percent had received at least one of these forms of government assistance (a breakdown by type of assistance was not provided by the GSS).

As can be in Figure 4.10, those who have received some form of government assistance show much higher levels of generosity overall than those who have not received assistance. Income awards given by people who have received assistance average slightly less than $270 per week--over $16 per week, and $65 per month more than the average award of $253 per week given by respondents who have never received such assistance (p < .01).

RESIDENTIAL LOCATION: GENEROSITY BY REGION AND CITY SIZE.

Regional differences in cost of living and in government assistance levels represent an important consideration when examining levels of generosity as represented in the GSS vignettes.

Figure 4.10
Generosity Level by Received Welfare

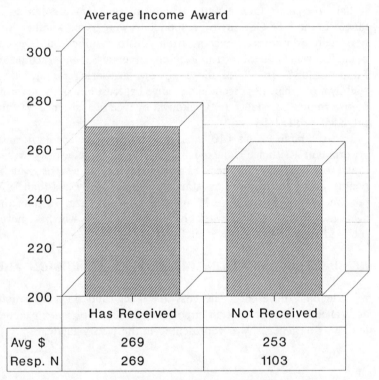

Average Income Award

| Avg $ | 269 | 253 |
| Resp. N | 269 | 1103 |

Ever Received Welfare

Avg $

Differences sig. p < .01

In Figure 4.11 the average weekly award by respondents' region of interview is presented.[7] As can be seen in Figure 4.11, in five of the nine regions of the country, there is virtually no difference in the weekly award given to the vignettes. These regions (N.E, MA, ENC, WNC, and ESC) average awards ranging from $263 per week to $265 per week. In only three of the regions is the average weekly award less than $250 per week (S.A., WSC, and MTN), with the lowest weekly award, $237, being found in the Mountain Region. Although these differences between regions are statistically significant (p < .01), the intra-regional variation is less than was anticipated. Of particular interest is the average award given in the East South Central Region, which includes Kentucky, Tennessee, Alabama and Mississippi. In this region respondents awarded the highest weekly award despite the region being notorious for the lowest assistance levels.

This point is best illustrated when comparing weekly awards to vignette families with the weekly AFDC payments for each region (see: *Statistical Abstracts of the United States*, 1989, p. 367). In Figure 4.11a, the average weekly award given to the vignettes is presented along with the Aid to Families with Dependent Children payments for each region.[8] Average AFDC payments are presented for the state with the highest AFDC allotment and for the state with the lowest allotment. As can be seen in this figure, the inter-regional differences in average vignette award between are completely overshadowed by the dramatic differences between **Vignette Award** and actual **Government AFDC Assistance**. When contrasted with the state payments, the slight dips in average award corresponds to a similar dip in average AFDC payments (with the exception of the ESC). For in every region the average vignette award is more than three times the award given by the lowest state average, and more than twice the amount allotted by the highest state average in each region except the PAC. In the East South Central, the average vignette rating is more than 10 times the award of the lowest state average.

Figure 4.11
Generosity Level by Region

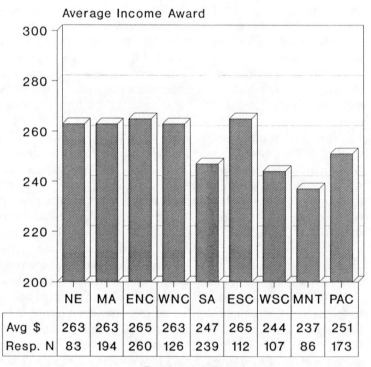

Average Income Award

	NE	MA	ENC	WNC	SA	ESC	WSC	MNT	PAC
Avg $	263	263	265	263	247	265	244	237	251
Resp. N	83	194	260	126	239	112	107	86	173

Region of Residence

▨ Avg $

Differences sig. p <.01
See text for states in each region

Figure 4.11a
Generosity/AFDC by Region

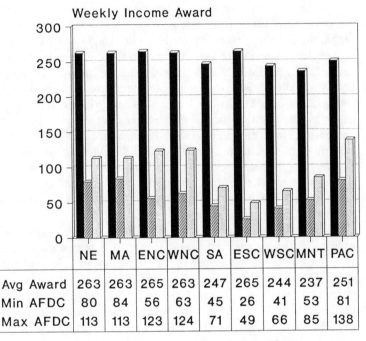

Weekly Income Award

	NE	MA	ENC	WNC	SA	ESC	WSC	MNT	PAC
Avg Award	263	263	265	263	247	265	244	237	251
Min AFDC	80	84	56	63	45	26	41	53	81
Max AFDC	113	113	123	124	71	49	66	85	138

Region/AFDC Awards

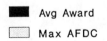

■ Avg Award   ▨ Min AFDC
▨ Max AFDC

Min=lowest state average in region
Max=highest state average in region

City Size and Generosity.

In addition to location of respondent residence, size of residence also represents a "political/ideological" component when examining levels of generosity toward the poor. In particular, the larger, more expensive the place of residence--and the prevalence of the more visible poverty relief programs--the higher the levels of generosity respondents would be expected to exhibit.

In Figure 4.12, the average income award for the size of the respondents' place of residence is presented. As can be seen in this graph, the average generosity level is quite closely related to the size of the place of residence. The highest levels of generosity are found in the 12 largest SMSA's in the country and the suburbs around those SMSA's, while the lowest average income awards are given by those respondents who live in rural areas. Although these findings were expected, the extent of these differences is less than was expected. As can be seen from the graph, the differences are only slightly significant ($p < .05$), with most of the overall difference, ranging from \$15 to \$30) being between rural and all others in the top 112 SMSA's and their suburbs. The middle categories for size of residence--the suburbs and the 13th through 112th largest SMSA's--show only marginal differences in income awards.

These findings were somewhat expected. In addition to the cost of living differences between, in particular, the largest cities and the rural areas, the predominance of non-whites in the cities rather than rural areas was also expected to elicit different overall levels of generosity. However, as can be seen in the graph, what marginal differences that are found still indicate a high level of overall generosity among all groups, and only slight variations between the majority of respondents--as represented in the middle 4 categories ranging from top 100 SMSA's to other urban areas.

Figure 4.12
Generosity Level by Residence Size

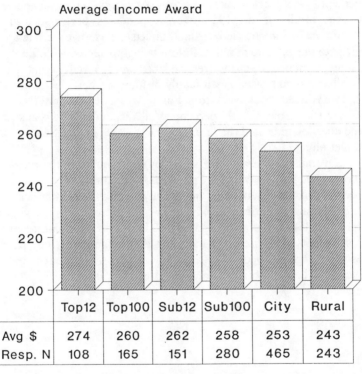

Average Income Award

	Top12	Top100	Sub12	Sub100	City	Rural
Avg $	274	260	262	258	253	243
Resp. N	108	165	151	280	465	243

Residence Size

▨ Avg $

Differences sig. p <.05

What it Takes to Get By?

In addition to taking into account the overall effect of the various respondent characteristics being shown toward the vignette families, we can also examine whether perceptions of what minimum income it takes for a family to live effect levels of generosity. Increased levels of generosity generated by empathy or sympathy as a result of respondent characteristics could also be affected by respondent perceptions of what it takes to get by. As can be seen when examining the results of the GSS survey, respondents' perceptions of the "minimum income needed" strongly affects the average income award given to the vignette families. Before being presented with the young family vignette scenarios, respondents were asked "What is the smallest amount of money a family of four (husband, wife, and two children) needs each week to get along in this community?" As can be seen in Table 4.2,[9] 94 percent of all respondents who answered the question indicated that a minimum of $200 per week was needed to get along.

Overall, the average assessment by respondents on the minimum income needed was over $354 per week--with almost 40 percent (39.0 percent) of the respondents indicating it would take $400 per week (the "average American weekly income" as presented in the vignette rating scale) or more for a family of four. Almost one-fifth of the respondents (18.6 percent) indicated that a family of four needed $500 or more per week to get by. Only six percent of the respondents indicated that a family of four could get by on less than $200 per week.

TABLE 4.2

Perceived Minimum Weekly Income Needed
For Family of Four

Weekly Income Needed	%
< $100	1.3
$101 - 150	4.1
$151 - 200	15.1
$201 - 250	11.6
$251 - 300	21.9
$301 - 350	6.6
$351 - 400	18.2
$401 - 450	2.6
$451 - 500	10.0
$501 - 600	3.2
Over $600 per week	5.4

Mean   354.34   Median   300.00

N = 1375

When we examine the relationship between the minimum income perceived by the respondent and the levels of generosity, the variations in levels of generosity for different levels of minimum income show strong support for the empathy/sympathy framework. As can be seen in Figure 4.13, the higher the income one believes it takes to get by, the higher the average level of generosity ($p < .000$). As can also be seen in Figure 4.13, the major gap in appears between those persons who see $400 or more as the minimum income needed for a family of four, average awards in excess of $274 per week, and those who believe the amount needed is less than $400, who average $256 or less in weekly income award to the vignette families. Note, however, that for even those respondents who believed that a family of four could get by on less than $200 per week, the average income award given to the vignette families was more than $238 per week.

Thus, again, we find that, when examining the overall levels of generosity shown toward the vignette families, there is strong evidence that, there exists an income "floor" below which few respondents believe anyone should fall and this floor is, for the most part, substantially higher than those levels which are covered by current government levels of support. Finally, there appears to be an underlying structure, referred to here as the empathy/sympathy factor, in which those who belong to social groups most at risk of falling into poverty (blacks, elderly, etc), those who may fit into circumstances similar to the characters depicted in the survey, or those who have experienced the effects of the need for support because of decreased income, show higher levels of generosity toward these fictitious families than those persons who do not have these characteristics.

However, the preceding presentation focused primarily on the overall relationship between the respondents personal and situational characteristics. Presenting the Analysis of Variance results comparing the average income award for the different subgroups of the population allows us to understand the general patterns of generosity. In the next section, the analysis will return to the examination of the individual vignettes in order to assess the independent effects of the respondent characteristics. In this way, a more detailed understanding of these characteristics will allow us to further examine the effects of the empathy/sympathy factors on levels of generosity.

Figure 4.13
Generosity Level by Income Need

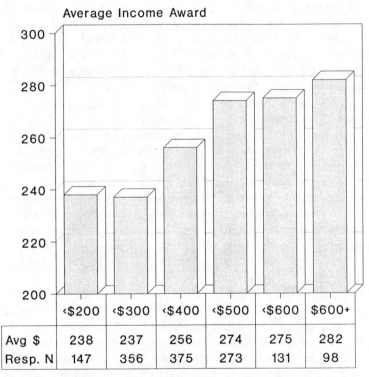

Average Income Award

	‹$200	‹$300	‹$400	‹$500	‹$600	$600+
Avg $	238	237	256	274	275	282
Resp. N	147	356	375	273	131	98

Minimum Income Needed

▭ Avg $

Differences sig. p ‹.001

ESTIMATING THE EFFECTS OF EMPATHY/SYMPATHY

To interpret properly the factors and their association with levels of generosity, we must examine the individual impact of those characteristics. Two dimensional, or bivariate analysis of variance comparisons allow for a general overall discussion of the effect various respondent characteristics may have on levels of generosity. It is not easily discerned from this analysis how those effects may be influenced by, or influence, the effects of other characteristics. The extent to which empathetic or sympathetic factors can be independently observed requires intervening effects to be held constant through multivariate analysis. In order for us to examine the independent effects of respondent characteristics on levels of generosity, multiple regression analysis is used.

To that end, those respondent characteristics that were considered to be important factors in examining the effects of empathy/sympathy on generosity were included in a regression model, using vignette income awards (i.e. vignette level awards) as the dependent variable. As can be seen in Table 4.3, mixed results were found when examining the effects of the empathy/sympathy factors on the levels of generosity shown toward the vignette families.

Several respondent characteristics were easily transformed into binary, or dummy, variables. For respondent gender, females were included in the equation, while male respondents were used as the reference group. Non-whites (which includes blacks as well as all "other races") were included in the analysis, with whites serving as the reference. Similarly, dummy variables were created for the various work status categories, with full-time employed individuals serving as the reference, and married people used as the omitted category for marital status with single, separated, divorced, and widowed respondents being placed into their corresponding binary variable. Region of residence and size of respondents city of residence also were included, with the omitted categories of Northeast and rural residents, respectively.

TABLE 4.3
Respondent Characteristic Effects
On Overall Vignette Level Ratings

Respondent Characteristics	B
Respondent Gender (male omitted)	
Female respondent	.69
Respondent Race (white omitted)	
Non-white respondents	34.94****
Respondent Age (Continuous)	.08
Presence/Age of Respondent's Children (over 6 omitted)	
No children	11.33***
Young babies present	12.05****
Respondent Education (grades completed)	1.91****
Respondent Marital Status (Married Omitted)	
Never married	15.18****
Separated	16.13**
Divorced	6.34#
Widowed respondent	-8.70*
Respondent Has Received Welfare	12.41****
Respondent Work Status (Full time employed omitted)	
Respondent works part time	.84
Respondent not working	7.78#
Respondent retired	31.44****
Respondent keeps house	7.53*
Respondent in school	- 8.41
Respondent Household Income	
(In $100, Continuous)	-.04****
Minimum Income Needed	.09****

T A B L E 4.3 (cont'd)

Respondent Characteristics (cont'd)	B
City Size (Rural Omitted)	
Top 12 smsa	1.73
Suburb in top 12 smsa	7.24
Top 100 smsa	3.99
Suburb in top 100 smsa	8.13*
Counties with cities with 10g+	11.54***
Region of Residence (Northeast Omitted)	
East North Central	-2.37
West North Central	9.99#
Mid Atlantic	-8.08
East South Central	.47
West South Central	-18.14***
South Atlantic	-14.57**
Mountain	-23.57****
Pacific	-16.80***
Vignette Characteristics	
Vignette Family Children	
Age of children	.29
Number of children	12.76****
Child's mother's education	.94*
Parent's Marital Status (parents married omitted)	
Mother divorced	.35
Mother never married	-.91
Father remarried	-1.23
Mother's Employment Status (employed omitted)	
Mother works part time	1.24
Mother looking for work	5.50#
Mother unemployed, only min. wage jobs	-19.18****
Mother unemployed, no child care	.84
Mother unemployed, not looking	-10.16**
Mother unemployed, no transport	-11.16**

T A B L E 4.3 (cont'd)

Vignette Characteristics (cont'd)	B
Father's Employment Status	
Father disabled	26.22****
Father unemployed, not looking	-7.23*
Father in prison	5.97#
Father unemployed, but looking	9.58**
Problems faced by family (problems next few months omitted)	
Problems for next few years	5.21*
Problems continually in future	2.98
Parental Assistance (parents help out omitted)	
Parents cannot help	.08
Parents could, but won't help	1.02
Parents would, she won't ask	-4.75
Vignette family income & savings	
Family's income	.38****
Family's savings	-.004#
(Constant)	90.59****

R Square	.210	
Adjusted R Square	.204	
N=8447		

#	=	.10
*	=	.05
**	=	.01
***	=	.001
****	=	.0001

Other variables were more easily included in the analysis as continuous variables. These included the age of the respondent (in years), the education of the respondent (total years of education completed), and respondent household income (recoded in order to accommodate the continuous scale[10]). In addition, the respondents perceptions of the minimum income needed to get by was also included as a continuous scale.

The number and age of children in the respondents household was not as easily included as those characteristics discussed above. Recall that the primary differences found when examining the overall effects of the number of children on level of generosity were between those with no children or those with young children, as opposed to those who have children who are school age or older. In order to examine the independent effect of not having children, or having young children, in comparison to having older children, two dummy variables were created. First, if the respondent had no children a variable was created. Second, for those respondents with children, and a child under six years of age was present in the household, a second "Young Babies Present" variable was created. Those with children all older than six years of age, are used as the reference group.

Finally, the dummy variable presentations of the vignette characteristics were also included in the equation. This inclusion allows us to more thoroughly examine the explanatory power of the effects of the vignette scenario, coupled with the effects of the empathy/sympathy factors.

The inclusion of these characteristics allows for a much larger explanatory power than merely including vignette dimensions and levels. Overall, including these variables allows us to explain more than 20 percent of the variance (Adj. R^2 = .210 p .0000). Thus, in this equation a large portion of the levels of generosity displayed by respondents can be explained by inclusion of the empathy/sympathy components with the vignette design in the equation. As can be seen in Table 4.3, however, several of the components associated with the empathy factors discussed above do not prove to hold up when other factors are controlled for.

First, when we examine the effects of the respondents gender on levels of generosity, there are virtually no differences in levels of generosity for men and women. When examining generosity at the aggregate, or individual respondent, level, women were found to be somewhat more generous than males (sig. p <.05), although this appeared to be primarily due to interaction between race and sex differences. When included in the regression model, however, women are only slightly more generous than men, and the small difference that does exist is not statistically significant. The differences found in the ANOVA appear, therefore, to be a byproduct of other influences in the respondent makeup.

In addition, difference in generosity in relation to the respondents age is not significant (at p < .1), and substantively small ($.08 increase in level of generosity per year of age). As can be recalled from Figure 4.2, generosity for the various age categories indicated a curve-shaped distribution, with both the very young, and the very old respondents being the most generous. The low magnitude of the difference in award for respondent age as shown in the regression coefficients in Table 4.3 is believed to be in part a product of this bimodal distribution. However, again the decreased magnitude appears to indicate that other influences are affecting any one-way analysis interpretation of the effect of respondent age on generosity.

A major indicator in support of the empathy factor's influence on generosity continues to be the race of the respondent. When holding all other influences constant, non-white respondents continue to award more than $34 per week in income assistance to the vignette families than white respondents (p < .0000). Non-whites, those who have the highest overall probability of falling into poverty and welfare, strongly reinforces the proposition that those most similar to the vignette scenario are most sympathetic to the plight of the poor families.

Vignette Similar Characteristics.

Confounding the empathy proposition put forth here, however, is the impact seen when we examine the number and presence of children in the respondents household. For as can be seen in Table 4.3, we still find that those persons without children are much more generous than those persons with school age or older children (all older than 6 years of age), an increase in award of more than $11 per week (p < .001). Respondents with children under the age of 6 in their household also show significantly higher increases in levels of generosity than those respondents with older children, with average

weekly awards increasing by more than $12. The increased financial
need for health care, feeding, and clothing associated with having
young children and infants, as expected, proved to be of primary
importance in estimating increased levels of generosity. The increased
levels of generosity for people with no children, however, appears to
be explained primarily by characteristics not included in this discussion or equation.

The empathy/sympathy perspective is further influenced when we
examine the current work status of the respondent. As can be seen
in table those who are most affected financially are also the most
sympathetic toward the fictitious families. Unemployed respondents,
and particularly those respondents faced with fixed incomes due to
retirement are by far the most generous--even when all other factors
are held constant. Indeed, when all else is held constant, retired
people show exceptionally high levels of generosity, exceeded in
magnitude, as discussed earlier, only by generosity levels displayed by
non-whites.

Note that other work status characteristics show a very different
impact when controlling for other influences than were shown in the
ANOVA discussion above. Of particular interest are those respondents who are in school and those who keep house. As we see in
Table 4.3, those who keep house show significantly higher levels of
generosity than full-time employed persons ($+\$7.53$ $p < .05$). In
addition, those respondents who indicated that they were still in
school show lower (although not statistically significant) levels of
generosity ($-\$8.41$). One interpretation of these differences, which
supports the empathy/sympathy proposition is that, by virtue of being
in the home and thus more directly affected by shortages in funds
and making ends meet, those persons keeping house are more
sympathetic to the plight of the family. Conversely, students who are
arguably less constrained by financial shortages because of the
availability of financial aid or parental help, have less in common with
the plight of the vignette families and are thus less inclined to show
sympathy for those persons.

When we examine the independent effects of respondent
education on levels of generosity, we again find significant differences
among respondents. Higher educated respondents show much higher
levels of generosity than lower educated respondents, awarding
almost $2 more per week to the vignette families for each year of

education completed (p < .0000). Note that this is a somewhat different finding than when education was examined at the aggregate level. As we see when we refer back to Figure 4.4, when we examine levels of generosity by the highest degree obtained by respondents, virtually no differences can be seen. However, after controlling for other factors, education of the respondent becomes a major indicator of increased generosity.

Increased levels of generosity associated with the empathy/sympathy factors can also be seen when examining the effects of marital status. Indeed, as can be seen in Table 4.3, those persons whose marital situation would appear to indicate the most vulnerability, in particular single (never married) individuals (+$15.18 p < .0000), those persons who are legally separated (+$16.13 p <.00), and those persons who are currently divorced (+$6.34 p < .1), show significantly higher levels of generosity than married persons. Widowed persons, however, show significantly lower levels of generosity than their married counterparts, awarding almost $9 per week less to the vignette families (p < .05).

Having experienced the hardships depicted in the vignettes also proved to be an important indicator of generosity. Those respondents who have received welfare benefits, in one form or another, at some time in the past also showed significantly higher levels of generosity than those who have never received public assistance. Former recipients awarded more than $12 per week more in income awards to the vignette families than non recipients (significant at p < .0001).

The effect of respondent income on level of generosity, the final respondent characteristics which can be matched with the vignette dimensions employed, also strongly supports the empathy/sympathy proposition discussed here. As shown in Table 4.3, as respondent household income increases, the level of support decreases significantly (p < .0000). Thus those whose income level is closest to that depicted in the vignette scenarios, and of the welfare recipient population in general, the greater the empathy/sympathy displayed and the income awarded.

What it takes: location and getting by.

In the previous section of this chapter, differences in the levels of generosity associated with the empathy/sympathy factors were presented for three items from the GSS that generally concerned what it takes to get by. In particular, these variables were the size of the city the respondent lives in, the region of the country in which the person lives, and what each respondent perceived as the minimum weekly income needed for a family of four to get by in the respondents area of residence. When these characteristics are examined independently of extraneous effects, several important, and in some respects contradictory, results are found.

As can be seen in Table 4.3, the higher the respondents' perceived minimum income needed for a family of four, the higher the level of generosity displayed by respondents ($p < .0000$). Thus, from the sympathy perspective, those persons who perceive the financial hardships for their area to be higher, also show increased levels of generosity for those who are disadvantaged.

However, somewhat contrary to this finding, the size of the city is inversely related to what was expected. That is, when compared to those who live in rural areas, respondents living in the nation's largest cities show virtually the same levels of generosity, when holding all else constant. Although all of the categories for city size included in the equation as binary variables indicate increased income awards for the vignettes, only those in smaller urban areas (counties with cities of 10,000 people or more) and those living in the suburbs of the 100 top SMSA's show significantly increased levels of generosity. One possible explanation for this, again, is that other social characteristics, particularly the minimum income needed to get by, and the race of the respondent account for much of the impact living in large urban areas has on generosity.

Finally, when we examine the variations by region of residence, we find that the empathy position is, again, supported somewhat. In particular, those regions where we find increased concentrations of single, non-white respondents, as well as those regions which are traditionally higher educated--The Northeast, and the "rust belt" of the West North Central (the Upper Mid-west)--show much higher levels of generosity than the South, South West, and the Mountain regions. The one anomaly to this pattern concerns the level of generosity displayed by the Pacific region. When controlling for all else, the Pacific--which includes California, Oregon, Washington, Hawaii and Alaska--awards almost $17 less than respondents in the Northeast ($p < .000$). This finding was somewhat surprising here in light of the increased cost of living for persons in California and

Hawaii, as well as the high level of benefits actually awarded in Alaska. Again, however, it is believed that these findings are best explained by other social characteristics, both included and not included in the model.

SUMMARY AND CONCLUSION

In the previous sections of this chapter, strong support on the aggregate and the vignette level exists for further development of the empathy/sympathy position. Non-whites, a group that is largely over-represented in the ranks of the poor, show much higher levels of generosity than whites. Respondents who do not have the security of a partner because of marital discord or having never married also show increased levels of generosity.

Respondents whose financial and social situation is more secure appear less generous to the vignette families than the less well off. Those respondents who have received welfare in the past are much more generous toward the vignette families than non-recipients. Those with higher incomes, and steady jobs, however, perceive the fictitious families' plight as less deserving of increased incomes. As people increase in age and leave the precarious situations associated with youth and childbearing behind, levels of generosity decrease. This decreased level of generosity is less structured than that of income and work status, and, on the aggregate, appears to be divided by cohort--the very young and very old, living in the most precarious positions are the most generous while those in their salad days with set careers are less generous.

Despite having uncovered what appears to be a major component of understanding generosity, however, additional components are sure to be equally important. In particular, the political ideology of the respondent and the various forms in which that ideology come into play represent important ingredients to study in the attempt to understand what drives generosity. In the next chapter, the analysis will turn to those political persuasion items, and attempt to outline the overall, aggregate impact such variables have on generosity. Also, those characteristics will be dealt with more specifically in order to examine the independent effects of the political makeup of respondents.

NOTES

1. Although each respondent was given 7 vignettes, some respondents did not evaluate each vignette in their packet.

2. Each respondent was given seven vignettes depicting young families. The "Average income award" represents the average rating given to the vignettes. In order to present the distribution in a manageable form, average awards were rounded to the nearest $10 increment.

3. Note, however, that the dimensions and levels used in the "old women" vignettes were very different than those used in the young family vignettes. Thus any direct comparison between the two vignette types is primarily limited to the overall levels of award rather than by comparing the effects of the various dimensions and levels.

4. Unfortunately, a comparison of the age of respondent and, for example a vignette family head from the same age cohort cannot be examined in this context. Age was not included as a dimension in the female headed family vignettes. "Young" in this context refers to those vignettes depicting mothers with children, whereas respondents were also given a set of vignettes depicting the circumstances of retired widows.

5. A note of caution is, however, needed here because of the limited number of separated respondents (56: 19 males and 37 females). The intention here is not to over state the statistical significance of these differences, but rather to use these differences for examining the empathy/sympathy effect.

6. Not working includes persons who were unemployed, and temporarily laid off, as well as those persons not in the labor force.

7. Region divisions are the same as used in the *Statistical Abstract Of The United States* (see any year edition). States included in each

region are: New England (NE) -ME, NH, VT, MA, RI and CT; Middle Atlantic (MA) NY, NJ, PA; East North Central (ENC) OH, IN, IL, MI, WI;West North Central (WNC) MN, IA, MO, ND, SD, NE, KS; South Atlantic (SA)DE, MD, DC, VA, WV, NC, SC, GA, FL; East South Central (ESC) KY, TN, AL, MS; West South Central (WSC) AR, LA, OK, TX; Mountain (MTN) MT, ID, WY, CO, NM, AZ, UT, NV; Pacific (PAC) WA, OR, CA, AK, HI.

8. AFDC award data was obtained from the *Statistical Abstract of the United States*, 1988. Data presented is for 1985. "Weekly" AFDC award represents monthly average taken from Statistical Abstract, divided by 4 (weeks).

9. Table 4.2 has been presented in condensed form in order to better present the information.

10. The actual income question used in the GSS asked respondents to indicate which category their household income fell in. For this analysis, respondent income war recoded so that the midpoint of the category (e.g. $12,500 for the $10,00 to $15,000 income range) was represented in actual dollar amounts.

CHAPTER 5

POLITICS, IDEOLOGY AND GENEROSITY

INTRODUCTION.

As we discussed in the previous chapters, "generosity" refers primarily to overall level of income awarded to vignette families. In the previous chapter, we found that differences in levels of generosity vary with certain respondent characteristics. In particular, non-white, lower income persons show higher levels of generosity compared to white, higher income respondents. Similarly, those who are not working or are retired show higher levels of generosity toward the vignette families than those who are active in the work force. Indeed, respondent subgroups bearing those demographic characteristics that most closely resemble those who are most represented within the poverty population exhibit higher levels of generosity as shown in income awards given to the vignette families.

Not all respondent characteristics, however, are as neatly and easily examined with regard to levels of generosity as the demographic characteristics examined in the last chapter. The extent to which segments of the public feel some sympathy for persons suffering from poverty is related not only to social position, but is arguably a result of political and ideological beliefs as well. In addition to experiential and empathic effects on levels of generosity, differences in ideology, including political party identification, "conservative-liberal identification, and attitudes and preferences about the priorities for government expenditures and efforts can also be expected to elicit varying levels of generosity.

POLITICS, IDEOLOGY AND GENEROSITY.

The extent to which ideological beliefs and political action effect levels of generosity toward the poor, one could argue, is played out in the electoral process of the American system. In theory, political parties and their representatives on the campaign trail seek to establish themselves as representatives of a particular, or set of particular, ideological stances on issues ranging from armaments to welfare expenditures. The voter, it would seem, only need align his or her self with that particular party or its representative which comes closest to a mirror image of his or her self. Liberals thus align with liberals, conservatives align with conservatives.

Indeed, much of the argument over government assistance to the poor is polarized by political ideology and loyalty. Anecdotal evidence aimed at eliciting sympathy or empathy in order to increase social welfare spending is employed primarily by the advocates of one side to wrench the hearts of voters and lawmakers; opponents of such spending often focus on the extent to which such aid impedes economic progress and taxes incomes in order to throw money at an undeserving, often characterized as lazy population. Yet, as was discussed earlier, little has been done to examine in depth the extent to which political and ideological interests conform to such alignments.

In this chapter, we will examine the extent to which those political and ideological beliefs and orientations are related to generosity toward welfare recipients. We will again be using the 1986 General Social Survey. The analysis will integrate both standard attitudinal items employed by the GSS as well as the Factorial Survey component of the GSS examined throughout the previous chapters to examine the relationship between respondent political belief and generosity.

First, items most closely related to political action, including voting behavior, respondents' political and ideological self alignment will be examined in relation to levels of generosity. How one votes, if he or she votes, and the extent to which respondents consider themselves to be liberal or conservative, will be used to examined how those differences are reflected in levels of generosity toward the vignette families.

Next, the relationship between ideology and generosity will be examined in light of attitudinal items that address respondent ideological perspectives. The second focus within this chapter will be on a battery of GSS items that assess the respondents' concerns and priorities with government spending, as well as their assessment of the responsibility of the government to assist the poor in this country, thus will be compared and contrasted with generosity toward the vignette families. This examination will include those concerns and priorities and the extent to which they are related to generosity exhibited toward the vignette families

Politics as Usual.

Perhaps the most anticipated variations are those to be found along political party lines and self identification by respondents on the liberal-conservative scale. If the political rhetoric of the various parties is any indication, the stronger one identifies with the Republican party, the lower the expected levels of generosity, while the stronger the identification with the Democrats the higher the expected levels of generosity. Similarly, those who place themselves more toward the liberal end of the self-reported liberal-conservative scale would be expected to show increased levels of generosity.

In order to assess political party identification, respondents were asked, "Generally speaking, do you usually think of yourself as a Republican, Democrat, Independent, or what?" If the respondents indicated that they were Republican or Democrat, a follow-up item asked "Would you consider yourself a strong (Republican/Democrat) or not a very strong (Republican/Democrat)?" If the respondents indicated that they were Independents, belonged to a different party, or indicated "no preference," a follow-up item was then presented asking "Do you think of yourself as closer to the Republican or Democratic Party?" These follow-ups, therefore, allowed for differences to be examined not only with regard to Democrats and Republicans, but also for a much broader range of strength of party identification as well.

Indeed, as can be seen in Figure 5.1 there is a strong break in the levels of generosity between Democrats and Republicans, although within-party differences are only noticeable among Democrats. Among Republican respondents, only small differences can be seen between "strong" Republicans and Independents leaning toward the Republican party, averaging $242 and $241 in average weekly awards respectively.

Figure 5.1
Generosity Level by Political Party

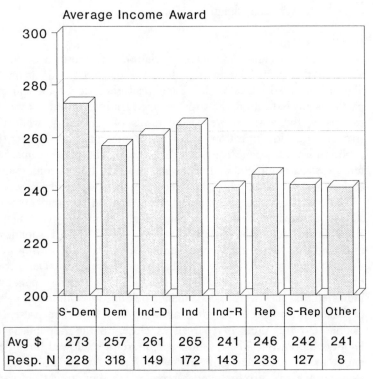

Average Income Award

	S-Dem	Dem	Ind-D	Ind	Ind-R	Rep	S-Rep	Other
Avg $	273	257	261	265	241	246	242	241
Resp. N	228	318	149	172	143	233	127	8

Party Identification

▨ Avg $

Differences sig. p <.001

Middle strength Republicans are slightly more generous than other Republicans, with average dollar awards of $246 per week. Those who stated they belong to other parties, although very few in number (eight) respond similarly to Republicans, with average weekly awards of $241.

Among those who identify themselves as Democrats, however, the average weekly award for strong Democrats is $16 per week more than middle-strength ones: $273 per week versus $257 per week. Independents leaning toward the Democratic party show slightly more generosity than middle strength Democrats, with average weekly awards of $261. The second most generous group of respondents, however, are those who consider themselves true independents, with generosity levels in excess of $265 per week.

Thus we find quite strong overall differences in levels of generosity between Democrats and Republicans, with strong Democrats averaging more than $30 more per week in awards than strong Republicans and more than $25 more than middle strength Republicans. True Independents and Independents leaning toward the Republican party are also significantly more generous than Republicans. In general, those who identify with Republicans, regardless of the strength of that affiliation, are less generous than all other respondents except those in other parties.

Party identification, however, appears to only be a partial measure for the effect of one's political persuasion on levels of generosity. In addition to party identification, respondents were also asked whether they considered themselves liberal or conservative. For this item, respondents were given a card containing a seven point scale ranging from 1, labeled "Extremely liberal," to 7 " Extremely conservative." Respondents were then asked to mark where they would place themselves on the scale. When we examine variations in average rating by the respondents' self-reported liberal or conservative position, we find that the primary differences exist only on the extreme ends of the liberal-conservative scale. In figure 5.2, differences in levels of generosity toward the vignette families is presented for respondents' self described political views.

Figure 5.2
Generosity Level by Political Views

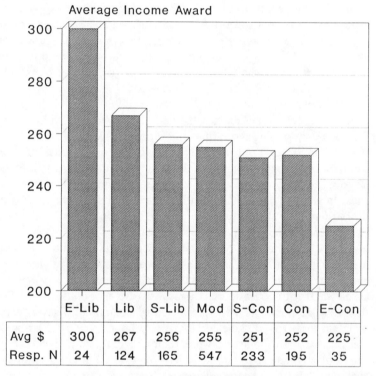

Average Income Award

	E-Lib	Lib	S-Lib	Mod	S-Con	Con	E-Con
Avg $	300	267	256	255	251	252	225
Resp. N	24	124	165	547	233	195	35

Political Scale

▩ Avg $

Differences sig. p <.01

As shown in Figure 5.2, only small differences are found between those who describe themselves as "slightly liberal" and "moderate" or those who consider themselves "slightly conservative" or "conservative"--with averages ranging from the low of $251 (slight conservative) to a high of only $256 (slightly liberal). On the other hand, extremely large differences of $75 per week can be seen between those who consider themselves "extremely liberal" and "extremely conservative"-- with averages of $300 and $225 per week respectively. Those who consider themselves "liberal" average $267 per week in award--more than $30 per week less than "extreme liberals," yet over $40 more than extreme conservatives. Note also that the actual number of persons who place themselves at either extreme is very small--less than 4 percent of all respondents--with the vast majority of respondents claiming to be either moderate or only slightly conservative or liberal.

Thus, as was expected, the more conservative the respondent, the lower the average weekly award given to the vignette families. The differences between Democrat and Republican respondents, as well as differences between those persons who identify themselves as liberals and conservatives, lend support to the ideological factor argument. Those persons who are more closely allied with conservative and Republican ideologies ARE less responsive to the need for government assistance than those who are Democrat or leaning ideologically toward the liberal end of the political spectrum.

Action versus Words.

When asked to identify party they belonged to, few respondents (i.e. less than .5 percent) refused to answer, although one third of the respondents indicated that they were independents, with a majority of those independents indicating that they leaned toward the Democrat or Republican party. Similarly, only five percent of respondents were not sure or did not answer when asked whether they were liberal or conservative. An important component to the impact of politics, however, is the extent to which citizens, regardless of party identification or political belief, actually partake in political process.

The 1986 GSS survey included three items aimed at assessing respondents' participation in the political process. First, respondents were asked whether they voted in the 1984 presidential election.

Respondents who voted were then asked to indicate who they voted for. For those not voting, or who were ineligible to vote, respondents were asked who they would have voted for if they had voted. The breakdown of respondent voting behavior is presented in Table 5.1.

As can be seen in Table 5.1, 70 percent of the respondents indicated that they voted in the 1984 presidential election. Slightly more than 3 percent of the respondents indicated that they were not eligible to vote, while almost 29 percent indicated that they did not vote for various reasons. Less than 2 percent refused to indicate or could not remember. Of those respondents who indicated that they did vote, 60 percent indicated that they voted for Republican incumbent Ronald Reagan, while 38 percent stated that they voted for Walter Mondale, the Democratic Party nominee.[1]

TABLE 5.1

GSS Respondent Voting Behavior
1984 Presidential Election

	GSS Survey		*US Total*	
Voted	66.9%		51.0 %	
Reagan		60.0%		58.8%
Mondale		38.2%		41.2%
Other/DN		1.8%		-----
Did Not Vote	33.1%		49.0%	

When we examine differences in levels of generosity toward the poor families depicted in the factorial survey vignettes, some important and somewhat unexpected results are found. In Figure 5.3, the average respondent generosity level is presented for the voting behavior reported for the 1984 presidential election. Two separate comparisons are presented in Figure 5.3: First, a comparison between those who voted and those who did not vote, and second between those who did not vote, those who indicated for whom they voted.

As can be seen in Figure 5.3, respondents who stated they did **not** vote in 1984 averaged significantly higher levels of generosity toward the vignette families than those respondents who voted. Non-voters averaged awarding $265 per week to the vignette families, more than $13 per week more in income awards than those given by those who did voted in 1984 (significance $p < .01$).

When differences between non-voters and voters for a particular candidate are examined, the results appear in more predictable form. For as can be seen in Figure 5.3, respondents who voted for Ronald Reagan in 1984 averaged only $240 per week in income awards, almost $30 less per week in awards to the vignette families than those who voted for Walter Mondale (average $268 per week), and $25 per week less than those who either did not vote, or those who voted for alternative candidates (each average $265 per week, significant at $p < .000$).

As was expected, therefore, the level of generosity expressed toward the vignette families does vary when comparison is made of the extent, and direction, of political activity, as seen in voting behavior. Somewhat unexpected, however, is the overall extent to which those who did not vote in the 1984 presidential election show higher average levels of generosity toward the vignette families than those who did vote, and even greater levels of generosity--more than $25 per week--than those who voted for Ronald Reagan.

Figure 5.3
Generosity Level by 1984 Vote

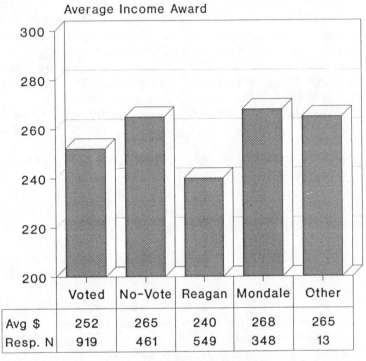

Average Income Award

	Voted	No-Vote	Reagan	Mondale	Other
Avg $	252	265	240	268	265
Resp. N	919	461	549	348	13

1984 Voting Behavior

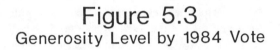 Avg $

Vote/No-Vote diff. sig. p <.01
No-Vote/Candidate diff. sig p <.001

THE ROLE OF GOVERNMENT: PRIORITIES AND RESPONSIBILITY

The General Social Survey included a variety of items to address the respondent's position on government responsibility for assisting the poor and items asking whether the government spends the right amount, too much, or not enough on various social problems.

Spending On Human Needs.

GSS items concerning government spending and responsibilities were presented in two basic forms. In one form respondents were asked whether the amount being spent on a particular program (e.g. space exploration, welfare, social security) is too much or too little. In the second form, respondents are asked whether the government should help in various situations (e.g. when persons are poor, or improving the standard of living), or whether the persons involved should "help themselves."

Respondents in the GSS project were asked a battery of questions concerning attitudes toward government spending programs. Interviewers presented respondents with a brief introduction, stating:

> "We are faced with many problems in this country, none of which can be solved easily or inexpensively. I am going to name some of these problems., and for each I would like you to tell me whether we are spending too much, too little, or about the right amount on...."

Respondents were then read a list of problems to rate.

In Table 5.2, the basic distributions for a selected set of the spending items associated with human needs is presented. Note that for the items on spending levels, several of the questions were worded differently for sub groups of the respondents. That is, for several items, different wordings were given to subgroups of the respondents in order to account for the effect of wording differences on response patterns.

In Table 5.2, several important patterns can be seen. First, we find that, for the most part, respondents feel that too little is being spent on areas of human need--improving the nation's health, dealing with drug problems, improving education, maintenance of social security, and improved assistance to the poor. Note, however, that respondents overwhelmingly indicated that the amount of money spent on international assistance was too great, and sizable numbers believe that too much is being spent to assist minorities.

As can be seen in Table 5.2, more than 60 percent of all respondents indicate that too little is being spent on health related issues in the US (either improving the nations health or more general health related issues). Only slightly more than 5 percent felt that too much public money was being spent on public health issues. Similarly, close to 65 percent of all respondents feel too little is being spent on education, with less than 5 percent stating educational spending was too high. Almost 60 percent of the respondents felt too little was being spent on Social Security. Sizable majorities also supported increased spending to combat crime (approximately 60 percent overall), and drug addiction and rehabilitation (approximately 55 percent).

Spending on other areas human needs and protection was, however, not as strongly supported by respondents. In particular, respondents were somewhat resistant to increased support for spending to help improve the conditions of black Americans, with roughly 20 percent of the respondents feeling too little was being spent, and large proportions feeling too much was being spent to assist minorities (28 percent to 43 percent, depending on how the question was worded). In addition, a vast majority of the respondents, 75 percent, felt that too much was being spent on assistance to foreign countries.

A second major pattern we find in Table 5.2, is that for some areas, particularly the broad areas of public assistance, assistance to cities, and improving the conditions of minorities, the wording of the item strongly affects respondent perceptions of whether too much or too little is being spent on particular social problems.

T A B L E 5.2

GSS Government Assistance Items

Item[2]	% Too Little	% Too Much
Health		
Improving Nations Health (n = 702)	60.7	4.1
Health (n = 707)	61.0	7.1
Cities		
Problems of Big Cities (n 651)	48.2	17.8
Assistance to Big Cities (n = 651)	17.7	38.1
Crime		
Halting Rising Crime (n = 693)	66.8	4.9
Law Enforcement (n = 705)	52.9	6.8
Drugs		
Drug Addiction (n = 695)	60.7	6.3
Drug Rehabilitation (n = 691)	52.9	6.8
Education		
Improving Nations Ed. (n = 705)	62.3	4.3
Education (n = 720)	67.5	5.1
Minorities		
Improve Conditions of Blacks(n = 691)	17.1	42.5
Assistance to Blacks (n = 688)	24.1	27.8
Int'l Aid		
Foreign Aid (n = 698)	6.4	73.5
Assistance to Other Countries(n = 706)	4.7	78.3
Public Assistance		
Welfare (n = 700)	23.1	42.0
Assistance to the Poor (n = 706)	62.8	9.3
Elderly		
Social Security (n = 1419)	57.1	6.3

Indeed, this is particularly prominent when examining public assistance, and assistance to cities, and when comparing question versions measuring the proportions who believe too much is spent on minorities. Smaller fluctuations in support for increased (or decreased) spending can be seen when examining different wordings for questions dealing with spending on law enforcement, drugs, and educational expenditures.

Wording for items addressing aid to large cities, half of the respondents were asked about spending to "solve the problems of big cities," while other respondents were asked about "assistance to big cities." As we see in Table 5.2, respondents asked about spending on assistance to big cities were far less supportive of such spending, with more than 38 percent stating they felt too much was being spent. In contrast, when asked about spending to deal with problems of big cities, more than 48 percent felt too little was being spent.

Similarly, a large proportion, more than 42 percent, of respondents asked about spending aimed at "improving the condition of blacks" felt too much was being spent. In contrast, less than 28 percent of respondents asked more generally about spending aimed at "assistance to blacks" felt that too much was being spent.

Of particular interest here, are the differences between respondents asked about spending on WELFARE and those asked about ASSISTANCE TO THE POOR. For those respondents questioned more generally about "welfare" a large proportion--42 percent -believe too much is being spent, while almost 2/3 (63 percent) of the respondents questioned specifically about levels of spending on "assistance to the poor" felt too little was being spent.[3] This appears to be almost a complete flip of opinion, merely by exchanging one word--changing the wording from "welfare" to "assistance."

Spending and Generosity.

In addition to examining the spending priorities of respondents, we can also we examine the relationship between those preferences for government spending and levels of generosity shown toward the vignette families. Indeed, when levels of generosity toward the vignette families are examined in relationship to respondents spending concerns, we find that those persons who favor increased spending towards human needs also show much higher average levels of generosity toward the vignette families. In Table 5.3, the average levels of generosity exhibited toward the vignette families is presented for respondents preferences for each of the spending items.

As shown in Table 5.3, for all of the human needs spending items, respondents who indicated that too little was being spent also averaged higher levels of generosity than those who felt too much was being spent, or believed spending on the particular items was about the right amount. In addition, with the exception of the items concerning spending on drug associated problems and law enforcement, as well as the more general assistance to other countries item under the International Aid category, those differences proved statistically significant. Respondents who felt too little is spent on problems facing big cites, and those favoring increased foreign aid, however, showed significantly higher levels of generosity than those who felt too much was being spent -ranging from $27 and $35 per week more in weekly awards for problems of cities and assistance to cities, respectively (each , p < .01), to more than $40 increase per week in income awards for respondents who believed too little was being spent on foreign aid (p < .001).

Of particular interest here, however, is the relationship between generosity level and spending priorities shown toward issues of health, education, welfare, and improving the conditions of minorities. As can be seen in Table 5.3, these areas show a particularly strong relationship between generosity and favoring increased funding for human services programs.

The strongest relationship found here is seen through examination of the level of generosity exhibited toward the vignette families and in attitudes toward government spending on assistance to minorities. As we can see in Table 5.3, those respondents who believe that too little is being spent to combat the problems facing minorities, award more than $35 more per week to the vignette families than those who believe too much is being spent on such assistance (p < .0001).

TABLE 5.3
Average Weekly Income Award for Vignette Families
For GSS Government Human Needs Spending Items

Item	Too Little avg $(n)	About Right avg $(n)	Too Much avg $(n) p
Health			
Nation's Health	$265(406)	$251(234)	$254(24)#
Health	$259(406)	$247(302)	$227(51)*
Cities			
Problems Cities	$270(299)	$252(213)	$243(108)**
Assistance Cities	$272(103)	$258(266)	$237(230)**
Crime			
Halting Crime	$261(441)	$258(183)	$253(33)
Law Enforcement	$257(359)	$252(220)	$244(44)
Drugs			
Drug Addiction	$263(402)	$252(217)	$255(42)
Drug Rehab.	$257(370)	$252(220)	$237(62)
Education			
Nation's Ed.	$264(415)	$255(225)	$229(28)*
Education	$257(458)	$247(186)	$234(36)#
Minorities			
Conditions Blacks	$279(229)	$249(297)	$240(109)**
Assist Blacks	$272(159)	$253(317)	$237(176)**
International Aid			
Foreign Aid	$292(42)	$274(131)	$252(486)**
Other Countries	$255(33)	$261(114)	$249(518)
Public Assistance			
Welfare	$278(156)	$260(230)	$249(279)**
The Poor	$259(423)	$245(187)	$236(66)*
Elderly			
Social Security	$261(773)	$253(482)	$230(85)**

= p <.01   * = P <.05 ** = P <.01

Indeed, this relationship holds for both versions of the minority assistance items. Respondents who indicated too little was being spent on assistance to blacks averaged more than $272 per week in income awards, whereas those who felt too much was being spent averaged slightly more than $237 per week in awards (p < .001). Similarly, respondents who believed too little was spent on "improving the conditions of blacks" averaged more than $39 per week more in income awards than those who believed too much was being spent (p < .0001).

Respondents who indicated that they believed too little was being spent on public assistance awarded approximately $25 per week more than those who felt too much was being spent--$29 per week more for those with the "welfare" question version (p .01) and at least $23 more for those asked about "general assistance" (p < .05). Similarly, respondents who believe that too little is being spent on Social Security also showed significantly higher levels of generosity than those who felt too much was being spent--averaging more than $30 more per week in generosity level (p < .001).

Who's Responsible for Change?

In addition to items that assess respondent perceptions about government spending on dealing with various social problems, a number of items were included to examine what respondents saw as the government's responsibility for helping poor citizens. In particular, respondents were asked whether the government should actively do something to reduce income differences between rich and poor citizens. In addition, later in the interview respondents were asked a battery of question concerning whether it was the government's responsibility to help with income maintenance and health programs or if individuals were responsible for helping themselves.

Respondents were presented with an item which presented two alternative perspectives on elimination of income inequality in the US. Respondents were told that "Some people think that the government in Washington ought to reduce income differences between the rich and poor, perhaps by raising the taxes of wealthy families and giving income assistance to the poor. Others think that the government should not concern itself with reducing this income difference..." Respondents were then given a card with a scale ranging from 1 to 7, with 1 indicating that "The government should do something to reduce income differences between rich and poor", and 7 stating " The government should not concern itself with income differences." Respondents were asked to indicate which "comes closest to the way you feel?" In Panel A of Table 5.4, the basic distribution for responses to the income redistribution item is presented.

As can be seen in Table 5.4, almost one third of the respondents indicated strong support for government actions to reduce income differences between rich and poor (i.e. answered either 1 or 2 on the 7 point scale), with less than 19 percent feeling strongly that the government should not concern itself with such matters (a '6' or '7' on the 7 point scale). A large proportion of respondents, slightly less than 50 percent, responded in the middle range of the scale, with the overall distribution skewed toward the lower, or more re-distributive end of the scale, with an average rating of 3.56 on the 7 point scale.

Thus only a small minority of respondents are strongly opposed to government intervention aimed at reducing income differences. A somewhat larger proportion strongly favor having government actively work toward the elimination of such differences. The largest proportion, although leaning toward strong government action, appear somewhat ambivalent about the extent of government responsibility for reducing income inequality.

Subsequent GSS items asked respondents more specifically about areas in which the government "ought," or "ought not" be involved. A battery of four items were presented to respondents to find out what areas were perceived as ones in which the government has responsibility for alleviating inequality. The questions were posed to show contrasting perspectives, stating "some people believe the government in Washington should.... Others believe that it is not the government's responsibility, and that each person should take care of themselves." Respondents were given a card containing a scale ranging from 1, which read "I strongly agree that the government should...", to 5, reading "I strongly agree that people should take care of themselves" on which to mark the position which came closest to his/her own beliefs. "I Agree with both answers," was printed above the 3, or midpoint, on the scale.

Respondents were asked to respond to four items. First, respondents were asked to respond to the statement that the government should "do everything possible to improve the standard of living of all poor Americans." Next, a more general statement stating that the government is "trying to do too many things that should be left to individuals and private business. Others think the government should do even more to solve our country's problems." Third, respondents were presented an item stating that it was the government's responsibility to "see to it that people have help in paying for doctors and hospital bills....."

Thus the first three items address health and welfare issues specifically. The fourth item in this battery asked respondents to respond to the statement "Some people think that blacks have been discriminated against for so long that the government has a special obligation to help improve their living standards. Others believe that the government should not be giving special treatment to blacks." For this item, the card presented a rating scale ranging from 1, "I strongly agree that the government is obligated to help blacks," to 5, "I strongly agree that government should not give special treatment." In Panel B of Table 5.4, the distribution of responses for the government responsibility items is presented.[4]

As can be seen in Panel B of Table 5.5, the most striking characteristic of the responses to those items concerning the government role in improving the standard of living in the US is the large proportion, almost 1/2 of the respondents, who stated that they agreed with both arguments--perhaps believing that responsibility for solving inequality and other problems facing the US was something both the government, and the private sector should do jointly. Approximately one third of the respondents favored increased government responsibility for improving the standard of living, while a similar proportion felt that citizens, and not the government, should do more to solve the social problems facing the United States.

T A B L E 5.4

Government Responsibility Items

Panel A: Reducing Income Differences

Reduce Income Differences[5]		%	N
Government should			
Reduce Income Differences	1	23.3	338
	2	9.0	130
	3	17.1	247
	4	20.9	302
	5	11.0	160
	6	6.1	89
Government Should not Concern itself	7	12.6	182

Mean   3.56   N = 1448

Panel B: Government Responsibility[6] to.....

	Improve Living	"Do More"	Med. Care	Aid Blacks
Government Should	31.3	26.3	49.6	18.2
Agree With Both	45.9	43.6	32.4	29.4
People Help Selves	22.7	30.1	18.0	52.3
Mean Response	2.8	3.0	2.5	3.6
Valid N	1430	1386	1427	1427

Respondents are less indecisive with regard to responsibility for health care and assistance to minorities. One-half of the respondents believe that it is the responsibility of the government to see that people can pay their hospital and doctor bills, while an additional one third believe that it should be at least a joint effort. Less than 20 percent (18 percent) responded that they believe people should take care of their own health care costs.

When asked whether the government, because of past discrimination and inequality, has a special obligation to assist blacks, however, the responses are quite different. As we can see in Panel B of Table 5.4, more than half, 52.3 percent, of the respondents indicated that they believe that NO special attention should be given to the problems facing blacks. Less than 20 percent (18.2%), on the other hand, indicated that they believed the government does have a special obligation to improve the living conditions of black Americans.

Responsibility and Generosity.

As we saw in the previous discussion of GSS items examining the perceived government responsibility for dealing with social problems, health and welfare issues, little consensus exists as to the proper role of the government. The marginal distribution of responses to those items shows a somewhat bimodal relationship, with, for most of the items, the majority of respondents seeing the solution to these issues as one of both government and individual concern.

When we examine the relationship between respondents perceptions of responsibility on the one hand and levels of generosity exhibited toward the vignette families, a less ambiguous relationship is found. As can be seen in Table 5.5, a much more linear, and sometimes dramatic, positive relationship can be seen when we examine the average weekly income award given to those vignette families and how respondents perceived the governments responsibility. In Table 5.5 the average weekly income award is presented for the responses to the government responsibility items discussed above.

TABLE 5.5

Average Weekly Income Awards for Vignette Families
For Government Responsibility Items

Panel A: Reducing Income DIfferences

Reduce Income Differences		Avg. Award (n)
Government should		
Reduce Income Differences	1	$265 (320)
	2	$268 (119)
	3	$264 (253)
	4	$259 (282)
	5	$245 (152)
	6	$237 (83)
Government Should	7	$237 (171)
not Concern itself		

Differences Sig. p < .0001

Panel B: Government Responsibility to.....

	Improve Living $ N	"Do More" $ N	Pay Med. Care $ N	Aid Blacks $ N
1 Gov.	$277 (247)	$278 (171)	$273 (390)	$291 (108)
2	$259 (169)	$264 (176)	$258 (271)	$272 (131)
3 Both	$257 (627)	$254 (572)	$253 (444)	$264 (395)
4	$241 (156)	$253 (213)	$228 (158)	$243 (248)
5 Self	$233 (147)	$239 (178)	$239 (82)	$244 (463)

All differences significant, P < .0000

In Panel A, the average award is presented for the item addressing the government's role in reducing income differences between the rich and poor. It indicates that respondents who are strongly supportive of government action toward eliminating income differences show significantly higher levels of generosity than those who believe the government should not be involved. Indeed, those at the re-distributive end of the scale average almost $30 more per week than their counterparts advocating that the government not be involved in re-distributive efforts (p < .0001).

Similarly, In Panel B we find that those who are most supportive of government involvement in Health and Welfare issues are significantly more generous toward the vignette families than are those who advocate non-involvement. Indeed, as is shown in Panel B of Table 5.5, for each of the responsibility items presented those respondents who advocate greater government involvement average at least $25 per week (when asked whether the government should "do more" about social problems) more than those advocating non-involvement (p < .0001).

Even greater differences were found when differences in generosity were examined for the remaining responsibility items. Advocates of government action to improve the standard of living for the poor average more than $30 more per week in awards to the vignette families than those who advocate no government intervention (p < .0000), while those who favor government coverage of health care costs for the poor average more than $35 more per week in vignette awards than those who advocate no government subsidization (p < .0000). Finally, those persons who believe that the government has a special obligation for helping blacks because of past discrimination show even higher levels of generosity than those who believe no obligations exist, averaging almost $40 per week more in income awards to the vignette families (p < .0000).

THE ROOTS OF INEQUALITY: PERCEIVED CAUSES OF RACIAL INEQUALITY.

A cursory examination of the *Statistical Abstracts of the United States*, as well as almost any issue of any journal in the social sciences shows that although in absolute numbers whites represent a majority of the poor population, blacks, who represent only about 12 percent of the overall population, are highly over-represented in the poverty ranks. Indeed, according to the 1989 Statistical Abstracts, almost one third (33.1 percent) of all blacks fell below the poverty line in 1987, whereas approximately 10 percent of whites are within the poverty range (*Statistical Abstracts of the United States*, 1989, p. 452). In addition, "poverty", as used in lay circles, is used interchangeably with "black" when talking about the effects of poverty. This seems the case both because of the frequently discussed information about the over-representation of blacks in the poverty ranks as well as because of media coverage and academic publications dealing with the conditions of the African American poor population in particular.

Although items useful for a thorough examination of whether "poor" is synonymous with "black" are not available in the General Social Survey, the GSS included a battery of items assessing respondents perceptions of the roots of racial inequality, and the over-representation of blacks in the ranks of the poor. Respondents were asked four questions assessing their understanding of the roots of poverty among blacks. A preamble was read to respondents before the items, stating "On the average, Blacks have worse jobs, income and housing than white people. Do you think these differences are...." Respondents were then presented with four subsequent causes, for each of which the respondent was to answer either "yes," (the reason stated was the reason for racial differences in jobs, income and) or "no."

Respondents were not asked to compare each of the four items, but rather four separate questions were posed to respondents. The reasons used in the items included: 1) "Due to discrimination; 2) "because most blacks have less inborn ability to learn; 3) blacks don't have the chance for education to pull out of poverty"; and 4) because "blacks just don't have the motivation or will power to pull themselves out of poverty." In Table 5.6, the distribution of responses to these items is presented.

TABLE 5.6

The Roots of Racial Inequality

"On the average, Blacks have worse
jobs, incomes and housing than white people.
Do you think these differences are ..."

	% Yes	% No	(n)
Due to discrimination?	44.9%	55.1%	(1422)
Blacks have less inborn ability to learn?	20.6%	79.4%	(1415)

Blacks don't have the chance for
    education to pull
    out of poverty?
	53.0%	47.0%	(1432)

Blacks don't have the
    motivation or will power
    to pull out of poverty?
	61.0%	39.0%	(1404)

As can be seen in Table 5.6 the most prevalent finding is that for those items dealing with "structural" causes of inequality, in particular the items concerning discrimination and lack of educational opportunity, respondents are almost evenly split between those who agree and those who disagree. First, with regard to structural effects, when respondents were asked whether they believed differences in conditions for whites and blacks was due to discrimination, slightly less than 45 percent (44.9 percent) indicated that they did believe that discrimination was the cause of inequality. More than 55 percent, (55.1 percent), on the other hand, stated that discrimination was not the cause of inequality. Even fewer differences in the distributions of responses were found when respondents were asked about educational chances. When asked whether they believed inequality in jobs and income were due to blacks "not having the chance" for the education needed to pull one out of poverty, 53 percent of the respondents agreed, with 47 percent stating that lack of educational opportunity was not a cause of inequality.

When we examine respondent perceptions of the causes of inequality, as seen in those items which are more closely related to individual or genetic characteristics, however, respondents are less evenly split. When asked whether economic inequality was due to the lack of motivation, or will power, on the part of most blacks, almost two thirds of the respondents--61 percent--agreed with the statement, while less than 40 percent of the respondents believed that lack of motivation was not the cause of inequality. A large majority of respondents, therefore, believe that, in short, "lack of will power" on the part of blacks is the cause of inequality between the races.

Similarly, large differences in opinion arose when respondents were asked whether inequality was "because most blacks have less inborn ability to learn." As can be seen in Table 5.6, approximately 4 out of 5 respondents (79.4 percent) did not believe inequality was a result of a lack of inborn ability. Only 1 in 5, 20.6 percent, of the respondents indicated that they did believe genetics was the cause of inequality.

As can be seen in Table 5.6, respondents, as a rule, do not believe that genetic inferiority is the reason for economic inequality between the races. However, less agreement about the roots of inequality can be seen when we examine those items which are personally based (lack of will power or motivation on the part of blacks), and even less consensus for those items which address more structurally based causes of economic inequality (discrimination or lack of educational opportunity).

Generosity and the Roots of Inequality.
Although little consensus on the part of respondents about the causes of inequality can be seen, an important consideration for this analysis is the relationship between the perceived causes of inequality, and the level of generosity exhibited toward the poor, as represented by the vignette families. In particular, do those respondents who see

the roots of inequality as structural, or outside the control of blacks, show higher levels of generosity than those who see the problem as a personal defect. In Table 5.7, the average weekly income award given to the vignette families is presented for each of the inequality items discussed above.

Indeed, as can be seen in Table 5.7, those who indicated that they believed economic inequality between whites and blacks was due to structural conditions (e.g. discrimination and/or lack of educational opportunity) are significantly more generous than those who indicated that they believed structural conditions were not to blame. Respondents who indicated that they believed inequality was due to discrimination averages $24 per week more in income awards than those did not believe discrimination was at fault ($268 per week to $246, p < .0000). Similarly, those persons who believed that inequality was a result of the lack of educational opportunity for blacks averaged over $17 more per week, awarding more than $264 per week to the vignette families compared to $247 per week awarded by those who did not believe inequality was a result of unequal education opportunity (p < .0000).

In addition, those respondents who believed that economic inequality was due to a lack of motivation or will power on the part of blacks exhibited significantly lower levels of generosity. Respondents who agreed that lack of will power was the principle reason for racial inequality awarded an average of $252 per week to the vignette families, while their counterparts awarded an average of slightly more than $262 per week to the vignette families (p < .05).

In contrast to the predicted differences between those who perceive inequality as resulting from structural situations, and those who attribute the inequality to lack of motivation, the differences in level of generosity exhibited by respondents who believed that inequality was due to inborn ability and their counterparts is less straight-forward. As can be seen in Table 5.7, those who believe differences in economic status are due to less inborn ability, or genetic inferiority, are actually MORE generous to the vignette families than those who do not believe that genetics are the cause (p < .10).

TABLE 5.7

Generosity and The Roots of Racial Inequality

"On the average, Blacks have worse
jobs, incomes and housing than white people.
Do you think these differences are ..."

	Yes	No	
	Avg. $ (n)	Avg. $ (n)	sig
Due to discrimination?	$268 (600)	$246 (740)	****
Blacks have less inborn ability to learn?	$263 (276)	$255 (1057)	#
Blacks don't have the chance for education to pull out of poverty?	$264 (710)	$247 (638)	****
Blacks don't have the motivation or will power to pull out of poverty?	$252 (814)	$263 (503)	*

```
****    = p < .0000
***  = p < .001
**   = p < .01
*    = p < .05
#    = p < .10
```

WORK AND MARRIAGE: THE EFFECTS OF WELFARE

In addition to examining the factors which may cause inequality, and how perceptions of those causes may affect generosity, it is also important to examine perceptions about the effects of welfare on welfare recipients. If the public believes, as conservative political rhetoric would have it believed, that welfare is detrimental to the populace, would levels of generosity then be decreased?

The 1986 General Social Survey included a battery of items addressing respondents perceptions of the effects of welfare. In particular, respondents were given six items which asked about the effects of welfare on work habits, marriage, and quality of life concerns. Before the battery of items, respondents were told that: "Here are some opinions other people have expressed about welfare. For each of the following statements, please tell me whether you..."[7] Respondents were then asked whether they agreed or disagreed with the statement, and how strongly they felt their position. Respondents were asked to answer statements including; 1) whether welfare makes people work less; 2) helps people in difficult times; 3) encourages young women to have children out of marriage; 4) helps preserve marriages; 5) prevents hunger and starvation; and 6) discourages pregnant women from marrying. In Table 5.8, the complete wording, and distributions of responses for these items is presented.

First, respondents were asked if they agreed to the statement that "Welfare makes people work less than if there wasn't a welfare system." Overall, 85 percent of the respondents agreed with the statement, 33.1 percent strongly agreed. Less than 2 percent of the respondents strongly disagreed that welfare makes people work less.

Almost an identical percentage of respondents (83.9 percent), however, also agreed when posed with the statement that welfare "helps people get on their feet when facing difficult times." Although only 12.6 percent strongly agreed with this item (as opposed to the 33.1 percent strongly agreeing to item 1), more than 71 percent agreed that welfare helps during hard times. In addition, only 2.9 percent strongly disagreed that welfare helps during hard times.

Thus respondents appear to be indicating that while welfare causes the poor to work less, they also believe welfare also gets people back on their feet when unemployed--somewhat contradictory stances, yet each equally strongly believed.

Table 5.8

Perceptions of the Effects of Welfare

"Welfare...."

	Strong Agree			Strong Disagree	
	1	**2**	**3**	**4**	
Makes people work less than if there wasn't a Welfare System?	33.1%	51.9%	13.2%	1.9%	(1452)
Helps people get on their feet when facing difficult times such as unemployment a divorce or death in the family	12.6%	71.3%	13.2%	2.9%	(1458)
Encourages young women to have babies before marriage	21.3%	40.0%	33.9%	4.8%	(1429)
Helps keep marriages together in times of financial problems	4.7%	54.3%	34.5%	6.5%	(1422)
Helps prevent hunger and starvation	15.6%	73.3%	9.3%	1.8%	(1460)
Discourages young women who get pregnant from marrying.	13.4%	46.7%	36.4%	3.5%	(1400)

Next, respondents were asked whether they agreed that "welfare encourages young women to have babies before marriage." Sixty one percent of the respondents agreed with the statement, that welfare encouraged women to have children before marriage, with 21.3 percent strongly agreeing. However, when posed with the next item, a large minority of the respondents disagreed that welfare encouraged out of wedlock children. Almost 40 percent (38.7 percent), of the respondents disagreed that welfare encouraged such child bearing practices, with 4.8 percent strongly disagreeing. When asked whether they agreed that welfare discouraged pregnant women from marrying,[8] an even larger percent (although still less than one half of the respondents) disagreed with the statement. Note, however, that more than 60 percent (60.1 percent) of the respondents agreed with the statement that welfare discouraged marriages for unmarried, pregnant women, with more than 13 percent strongly agreeing.

Next, respondents were asked about the effects of welfare on holding families together. Respondents were asked whether welfare "helps keep marriages together in times of financial difficulties." As can be seen in Table 5.8, a majority of respondents agreed with the statement, but only a small percent (4.7 percent) strongly agreed that welfare helps keep marriages intact. More than forty percent, however, disagreed that welfare helps preserve marriages, with almost 7 percent (6.5 percent) strongly disagreeing with such assumptions.

Finally, respondents were asked to respond to the statement "welfare helps prevent hunger and starvation." As can be seen in Table 5.8, a vast majority of respondents, 88.9 percent, agreed that welfare prevents hunger. More than 15 percent strongly agreed. Note, however, that one in nine respondents (11.1 percent) disagreed with the notion that welfare even had the positive effect of reducing hunger among America's poor population.

As can be seen in Table 5.8, therefore, it appears that, for the most part, a majority of respondents tended to agree with ALL of the statements about the pro's and con's of welfare. That is, whether presented with items showing critical problems from the effects of welfare, or items showing the benefits of welfare, a majority of respondents tended to support those statements--even if some of those statements were contradictory in nature.

GENEROSITY AND PERCEPTIONS OF WELFARE.

In analyzing the responses to these items assessing respondents perceptions of the effects of welfare, we can look at responses to the two perspectives designed in the battery of items. First, three of the items would seem to indicate that welfare serves its primary purpose of protecting those persons who are most vulnerable--the hungry, the unemployed, and the financially distraught. On the other hand, the three remaining items, when agreed with, indicate a less admirable welfare system in which people are encouraged to work less, and to discard the fundamental middle class family obligations of marrying before parenting. As we discussed in the previous section, however, the tendency for a large majority respondents in answering each of the "welfare effect" items, was to agree, or strongly agree to each statement, with only small proportions of the respondents ever strongly disagreeing with any of the items.

Yet when we examine the average weekly income award given to the vignette families by the responses to these items, strong differences in levels of generosity are found. Indeed, those who view welfare as more beneficial to recipients, and less debilitating on the morale and motives of those recipients, show much higher levels of generosity toward the welfare families depicted in the vignettes than their counterparts. In Table 5.9, the average income award is presented for the responses given on each of the welfare items discussed above.

As shown in Table 5.9, significant differences in levels of generosity can be seen for all of the welfare effect items. In fact, distinct patterns are found with regard to whether respondents perceive welfare as a beneficial program, or one that creates malcontents among the poor population. For each of the items in which welfare is shown as beneficial to the poor, respondents who agree with the statement show much higher levels of generosity. Respondents who strongly agreed that welfare helps get people on their feet during bad times averaged almost $15 per week more than those who disagreed with this statement, and more than $50 more per week than those whose strongly disagree ($p < .01$). Those who only agreed or disagreed, however, averaged awarding equal amounts to the vignette families, $256 and $254 per week, respectively. Similar differences were found with regard to the effect of welfare on preventing hunger. For this item, respondents who strongly agreed that welfare prevents hunger averaged more than $50 per week in awards to the vignette families than those who strongly disagree ($276 per week and $223 per week, respectively). Again, however, those respondents who only agreed or disagreed showed similar levels of generosity, averaging slightly over $253 per week for each response group. Overall differences in levels of generosity for the responses to this item were, however, statistically significant (p < .001).

In addition, those who strongly agreed that welfare keeps marriages together during hard times averaged more than $50 per week more than those who strongly disagreed, although the total number of those who strongly disagreed was quite small ($281 per week as compared to $230 per week), and $30 more per week than those who only disagreed. The middle categories (the straight agree and disagree responses) were separated by just over $9 per week in income award to the vignette family, slightly more than $260 and $251 per week, respectively. (overall differences significant, p < .001).

When we examine responses to those items that portrayed welfare as less than benign intervention, similar differences in levels of generosity are found, although the direction of the differences changes. That is, as can be seen in Table 5.9, significant differences in levels of generosity are also found when we examine those items which portray welfare as "demoralizing," although for these items those persons who agree show, for the most part, significantly LOWER levels of generosity than those who disagree.

First, when we examine average income awards given to the vignette families, those who agree that welfare makes people work less show significantly lower levels of generosity than those who either disagree, or strongly disagree. Indeed, those who strongly disagree that welfare makes people work less average almost $70 per week more in income awards than those who strongly agree with this position ($313 per week and $244 per week, respectively), and almost $60 per week more than respondents who agree ($255 per week). Those who simply agree average $280 per week in awards, $25 per week and $36 per week in income awards more than those who agree and strongly agree (respectively) that welfare makes people work less. These differences are highly significant (p < .0000), although the total number of those who strongly disagree is somewhat small.

Table 5.9

Average Weekly Income Award To Vignette Families
By Perceptions of the Effects of Welfare

"Welfare...."

	Strong Agree	Agree	Disagree	Strong Disagree
	Avg. $ (n)	Avg. $ (n)	Avg. $ (n)	Avg. $ (n)
Makes people work less than if there wasn't a Welfare System?	$244 (456)	$255 (708)	$280 (179)	$313 (25)
Helps people get on their feet when facing difficult times such as unemployment a divorce or death in the family	$268 (167)	$256 (983)	$254 (184	$215 (45)
Encourages young women to have babies before marriage	$243 (298)	$252 (537)	$264 (461)	$297 (64)
Helps keep marriages together in times of financial problems	$281 (66)	$260 (726)	$251 (465)	$230 (85)
Helps prevent hunger and starvation	$276 (211)	$253 (1010)	$253 (130)	$223 (24)
Discourages young women who get pregnant from marrying.	$252 (181)	$250 (616)	$264 (479)	$255 (45)

All within-group differences significant at $p < .01$ except where noted.

Differences in levels of generosity were similarly strong when examined in light of responses given when respondents were asked whether they agreed that "welfare encourages young women to have babies before marriage." For as we can see in Table 5.9, respondents who strongly disagreed with this statement averaged $297 per week in income awards, almost $55 more per week in awards than those who strongly agreed ($243 per week), and $45 more per week than the $252 per week average for those respondents who simply agreed that welfare causes out of wedlock parenting behavior (p < .0000). Respondents who disagreed with the assertion that welfare encourages "illegitimate" births averages $264 per week.

Note, however, that response patterns for all of the welfare effect items do not show the same patterns of generosity toward welfare families. The one exception to the pattern of differences in generosity for those who see welfare as beneficial and those who see welfare as less than benign is found when comparing generosity levels of responses to the statement that "welfare discourages young women who get pregnant from marrying the father of the child." For as can be seen in Table 5.9, differences in average weekly income award do not display a direct pattern as found in the other items, but rather fluctuates.

Although the overall differences that are found are statistically significant when analyzed using ANOVA (p < .05), respondents who strongly agree that welfare discourages marriage actually show slightly less average weekly income awards than those who strongly disagree ($252 and $255 per week, respectively) and those who simply agree with the statement ($250 per week). In addition, those who strongly disagree that welfare discourages marriage average $9 per week less than those who merely disagree ($264 and $255 per week, respectively).

As can be seen in table 5.9, therefore, we find that although response patterns appear to lean toward agreeing with each of the items that address the positive and negative effects of welfare, a strong pattern can be seen between the extent to which welfare is seen as positive or negative, and the levels of generosity exhibited toward welfare recipients. From all indications given in these items, respondents who find welfare more beneficial are much more generous than those who see welfare as problematic.

POLITICAL IDEOLOGY AND GENEROSITY: VIGNETTE ANALYSIS AND INDEPENDENT EFFECTS.

Throughout the preceding discussion of the variations in generosity and political ideology, each ideological characteristic was examined for individuals and compared for respondents average weekly income award. We examined various sets of items to gain a more complete understanding of respondent ideology from which these comparisons of generosity can be made. However, we need a more thorough examination of the effects these ideological perspectives have on generosity. To this end, in this section regression analysis will be used in order to examine the independent contribution each of the various ideological indicators offers toward modeling generosity toward the vignette welfare families.

As was discussed above, each of the ideology items was presented as part of a battery of scale items. By design, these items can then be combined into indices. For our purposes here, these indices can then be examined in relation to their effect on generosity toward the welfare families depicted in the GSS vignettes.

Index Construction: Political Ideology, Party Affiliation.

As can be recalled from the first section of this chapter, large differences in generosity were found between those who identified with the Democratic Party and those who identified with the Republicans, or other third parties. Democrats and true independents showed much higher levels of generosity than Republicans and third parties. Even more drastically, a strong, negative linear relationship exists between political ideology and generosity, with generosity decreasing the more conservative the respondents perceived themselves.

When we examine the relationship between these items, however, we find that they are less strongly related than we would anticipate. In particular, a straightforward zero-order correlation between political ideology and party identification reveals a Pearson R of only .31. In addition, a reliability test of relationship between the items to be used in construction of an index yields a Cronbach's Alpha of only .431--almost half the preferred values desired for scale construction.

Theoretically these items still represent important component of understanding generosity and support for welfare programs, and thus inclusion in the analysis is warranted despite some shortcomings in empirical reliability. In order to integrate these items into a more thorough analysis of generosity, the party identification and liberal-conservative measure were combined into a single additive index--a new index was created, therefore, by adding together the respondents' score on the party identification item and the liberal/conservative scale item. Thus respondents who indicated they belonged to a third party (the least generous category) and indicated that they were extremely conservative would receive a score of 15. Extremely liberal, strong Democrats, on the other hand, would receive a score of 1 on the Political Affiliation Index.

Spending Priorities.

As discussed in the previous section, respondents were asked a battery of items assessing whether they believed government spending on a variety of "human services" was too much, too little, or about the right amount. For a majority of these items two wording versions were used as part of an on-going effort in the GSS to examine the effect of wording differences on response patterns. Thus, although all respondents were asked about the spending levels for social security, when questions addressed public assistance spending, one half of the respondents were asked about "welfare" while the other half were asked about "assistance to the poor."

In order to examine these spending items as an index of support for human services, therefore, a straight additive index would not useful, or easily achieved. First, because of the fact that not all respondents received each question version, such a scale would actually render two somewhat different scales--one for each wording pattern. Mechanically, these two scales would not be useful because of problems of missing data which would, through list-wise regression, omit all cases if used in the same model.[9]

In addition to concerns with combining differing word patterns an additive combination of these items poses some problems because of the low correlation shown between items within each subgroup of respondents. Indeed, the average inter-item correlation for each group of these items is only .15, with no two items showing a Pearson R of greater than .39. In addition, when we examine the Cronbach's Alpha coefficient, used to determine the reliability of using these items as an additive scale, we find only slightly greater the .60 and the .64 Alpha level achieved for the two wording versions, respectively--

somewhat lower than the .80 (approximately) that would be preferable for such an index.

This is not to say that use of the items is not recommended. The primary purpose of these items was to examine the relationship between generosity shown toward the welfare families depicted in the vignettes, and the respondents' perceptions of funding levels on human services programs. To examine this relationship, we constructed an index measuring the extent to which "TOO MUCH" was believed spent on human services. To this end, an index was created by counting the number of times respondents indicated that TOO MUCH was being spent on a particular service. If a respondent indicated that too much was being spent on each of the services, a total score of 9 was calculated. If a respondent never indicated that too much was spent (indicating instead that too little, or the right amount was spent) the total score would be zero.

Government Responsibility Index.

The battery of General Social Survey items included above that addressed respondents' position on the governments role in dealing with general problems facing the country also allowed for construction of an Government Responsibility index. These items include whether the government should do more to solve social problems, reduce income inequality in the United States, and those items assessing whether the government should do more to improve the standard of living for the poor, provide medical care, and provide special assistance to blacks in order to atone for past discrimination (see table 5.4).

In order to utilize these items in the analysis of generosity, an additive index was constructed. Although the Cronbach's Alpha found when examining the overall reliability of these items is somewhat modest (Alpha = .629), the overall correlation between the items is much stronger than for items included in any other ideology index discussed here. Indeed, among these items, only in two instances, when correlation between the government's responsibility for reducing income differences and both the item assessing the government's role providing health care and in helping blacks, does the Pearson R fall below .25. The average inter-item correlation is .28. The additive Responsibility index ranges from 5, representing those persons who strongly agreed that the government had a responsibility to assist the poor and reduce inequality, to 27, representing those respondents advocating that the government has NO responsibility in these areas, and that people should help themselves.

Roots of Inequality.

The previous analysis included four items that addressed respondents' agreement with various reasons that have been put forth for the prevalence of blacks in the poverty ranks. The reasons cited in these items included discrimination, genetic differences, lack of educational opportunity and lack of will power on the part of blacks. Again, however, these items are being included as an index because of strong theoretical reasons, and less because of the items show a strong relationship with each other. Indeed, the average inter-item correlation for these items is small, only .196, and the test of reliability yields a Cronbach's Alpha of only .501, much smaller than would be preferred. Because of the very strong differences in levels of generosity shown between those who agree and disagree with each of these statements (see Table 5.7), the inclusion of this scale is warranted.

In order to create an additive index of these items, item 2 (genetic) and 4 (lack of will power) were recoded so that for each item the higher the score, the stronger the respondent felt that the roots of poverty in the black community was due to a problem or predisposition on the part of BLACKS rather than a social or structural base. The resulting scale ranges from 4, representing those who believe structural causes are at the root of racial inequality, and 16, representing those respondents who believe that personal characteristics of blacks are more to blame.

The Effects of Welfare.

The final ideology index to be included in this analysis is assesses the extent to which respondents believe welfare is beneficial or detrimental to those who receive assistance. These items were specially designed for comparative uses with the 1986 GSS and vignette supplement. Six items were developed and included in the GSS, assessing whether respondents believed welfare: 1) made people work less; 2) helped in times of unemployment; 3) encouraged the birth of children out of wedlock; 4) helped preserve marriages in hard times; 5) prevents hunger and starvation; and 6) discouraged marriage in cases in which a woman was pregnant.

As shown in the earlier discussion (see Table 5.8), three items, (1,3 and 5) were designed so that the stronger the respondent agreed with the statement, the more detrimental welfare was considered. Again we find that although specially designed for scale construction, these items show are only moderately related to each other. The average inter-item correlation is only .18. When testing the reliability of using these items for constructing a Welfare Value index, we are left with a somewhat small Cronbach's Alpha of .57--stronger than some other index measures presented in this section, but weaker than others. Again, however, because of theoretical and design consider-ations, an additive scale utilizing these items is warranted.

In order to construct the Welfare Effects index, the three items that portrayed welfare in a negative light were recoded so that the higher the score, the less detrimental the respondent considered welfare's effects on recipients. When added together, the Welfare Index ranges from 6, representing those persons who strongly believed that welfare was always detrimental to those who receive aid, to 24, representing those who believed that welfare was always beneficial to those who received aid.

Generosity and Measures of Ideology.

The primary purpose of constructing these indices was to examine the relationship between generosity exhibited toward the poor and respondents overall perspective on a political issue--in the case of these indices several sets of items assessing the general area of welfare. As we saw in the first part of this chapter, significant differences in levels of generosity were among respondents indicating opposite opinions for most of these items. In order to examine the extent to which each of these indices affects generosity, independent of other political items, we regressed the average weekly income award given to the vignette families on each of the political ideology scales constructed in the last section. Table 5.10 presents the coefficients for each of the ideology scales produced in the multiple regression analysis with the average weekly income award.

As shown in Table 5.10, however, not all of these indices proved to be important indicators of generosity toward welfare recipients. In particular, we find that the political ideology scale (an additive measure with the higher scores indicating conservatism and belonging to the Republican party), has virtually no effect on the overall levels of generosity exhibited toward the vignette families. Although the coefficient for the Political scale is negative, only marginal changes appear for increases in conservative affiliation.

Similarly, we find that those who believe that the root of poverty for blacks is more or less of their own volition and not a structural condition of society show lower levels of generosity. Again, however, these differences are only marginal, and are not statistically significant at any acceptable (i.e. $p < .1$ or $p < .05$) level. Those persons responding at the extremes for this scale differ in their average weekly income awards to the vignette families by less than $5 per week. One the other hand, three of these ideological indices DO show significant influence on generosity when all other political scales are controlled for. In particular, the extent to which one believes welfare is beneficial, beliefs in the government's responsibility for dealing with inequality (or non-belief in that responsibility), and, to a lesser extent, the extent to which one supports (or does not support) government spending on human services programs, all significantly influence generosity toward the poor.

The strongest relationships between generosity and political ideology are those found when we examine the Welfare Item scale and the Government responsibility scale.

As shown in Table 5.10, the more respondents agree that welfare is primarily beneficial, the higher the average income award they give to the vignette families. For each point increase on the 18 point scale (ranging from 6 to 24), and holding all else constant, an additional $4.26 was given to the welfare families--a change in award of more than $75 between the extremes of this scale (increases significant at $p < .001$).

Similarly, the stronger the belief that the government has NO responsibility to help eliminate income inequality or improve the living conditions of the poor, the lower the average income award given to the welfare families. For each increment increase in the 22 point responsibility scale (which ranges from 5 to 27), respondents average income award decreased $2.74, resulting in average income award differences of more than $60 per week between those persons who strongly believe that the government DOES have the responsibility to eliminate inequality (significant $p < .001$).

Table 5.10
Multiple Regression Analysis
Generosity Regressed on Political Ideology Scales

Political Scale Item	B
Welfare Beneficial (high = beneficial)	4.26****
Political Ideology Scale (high = con-rep)	-.60
Roots of Poverty Scale (high = blacks fault)	-1.14
Spending Priority Scale (high = too much)	-4.14*
Gov. Responsibility Scale (high = none)	-2.74****
(Constant)	252.62****

R Square	.076
Adjusted R Square	.072

N =   1070

#	= p < .10
*	= p < .05
**	= p < .01
***	= p < .001
****	= p < .0001

When we examine the coefficient for the Spending Priority scale, the pattern continues to be seen that support for government involvement, and belief in the benefits afforded by government programs are the strongest indicators of increased generosity. As evident in Table 5.10, respondents who believe too MUCH is being spent on government human services programs show significantly LOWER levels of generosity than those who believe spending levels are either too small or currently adequate. Indeed, for each point increase on the 10-point scale (range from 0 to 9), the average income award DECREASES by $4.14, a difference of more than $40 when comparing the extreme values on the scale. (significant at p < .05).

As can be seen in Table 5.10, the most important ideological factors that affect generosity concern the perceived quality of government welfare programs and the extent to which the government is viewed as responsible for dealing the nation's social problems. Respondents who perceive the programs as effective, and a part of the government's responsibility display much higher levels of generosity than those who support a "hands off" style of government. Political party affiliation and the extent to which one is liberal or conservative, when examined independent of other ideological factors, show little effect on generosity toward the poor.

In addition to the effects of each of the scale items on generosity levels, inclusion of these items also allows us to look at the broader picture and examine the overall effect that ideology (as measured above) has on generosity. As can be seen in Table 5.10, overall, the inclusion of these ideology scales allows us to explain more than 7 percent of the overall variance in the average income awards (R^2 = .076). Although this is not an overwhelming proportion, this represents only the effect of the available ideological items on generosity, without taking into account the relationship between individual respondent characteristics and generosity (discussed in the last chapter), or the variation in generosity found when examining the effects of the characteristics of the welfare families depicted in the vignettes (Chapter 3).

Political Ideology, Social Standing, and Generosity.

Through out this chapter, we examined the relationship between political ideology, as measured by various items examining different aspects of public assistance, and generosity toward welfare families. In addition, the analysis presented in the previous chapter, the relationship between generosity and the respondents social standing including basic demographic characteristics as well as geographic differences. It is important to remember that in many instances, political persuasion and social characteristics are inter-related. Wealthier respondents are more likely to identify with conservative causes, while highly educated and minority segments of the population ally themselves more frequently with liberal causes.

To conclude the examination of the roots of generosity it is necessary for both of these components--social standing and the ideological beliefs of the respondents--to be examined simultaneously in order to understand more fully the impact of each. To this end, we return to the vignette level analysis, where the weekly income award given to each vignette scenario was regressed on all of the respondent characteristics examined in Chapter 4 (see Table 4.3), and each of the political ideology scales discussed in the previous section.

The results of this multiple regression analysis are presented in Table 5.11, which shows that although many of the respondent social and political characteristics included in the regression did not prove to be statistically significant, those items that did prove significant offer an important blueprint for mapping generosity.

The clearest and strongest finding in Table 5.11 is that those persons who are most susceptible to the effects of poverty also show the highest levels of generosity toward the welfare families depicted in the vignettes. Nonwhites average awarding more than $17 per week more in awards than whites when controlling for all other influences ($p < .05$). Similarly, families with young children award more than $14 more per week than those persons with older children present ($p < .0001$), while those respondents with no children average slightly less than $10 more per week ($p < .01$). Also, we find that more highly educated persons are more generous ($p < .001$).

Not all of the personal hardship indicators, however, prove to be important with regard to overall generosity. Of particular note here, is that when we include the scale measures of the respondents political ideology, those persons who have received welfare in the past are only marginally more generous than those who have not received assistance. Indeed, the magnitude of the effect of receiving welfare on generosity was reduced by more than 80 percent, dropping from more than $12 when political variables are included, to slightly more than $1 in the present equation.

Those who are in the most vulnerable positions with regard to marital status, however, show higher levels of generosity than married people. Respondents who have never married and those who are separated give much higher weekly income awards, averaging more than $13 and $20 per week, respectively, in weekly income award to the vignette families than married respondents (each at p < .001).

Divorced respondents averaged more than $5 more per week in income awards, although this is not statistically significant. Note, however, that we once again find that respondents whose spouses have died show much lower levels of generosity toward the welfare families, averaging almost $20 per week less than married respondents (significant at p < .05). Again, these differences are found while controlling for other characteristics.

In contrast to widowers we find that retired persons show the strongest effect on generosity with regard to respondent social standing. Indeed, respondents who are retired award more than $35 more per week than those who work full time (p < .001). Also, note that the regression coefficient for respondent age is now positive (and significant at p < .05), whereas in the previous chapter when we examined age, without controlling for political persuasion, it appeared that the older the respondent, the lower the level of generosity.

When controlling for respondent social standing, we still find that those who believe welfare is beneficial show much higher levels of generosity toward the vignette families, averaging an increase of more than $4 per point on the scale (p < .001). Also, respondents who believe that the government is responsible for taking care of the poor and the infirm show much higher levels of generosity than those supporting the hands off style of government (p < .001). Note, also, that the magnitude of the coefficient for the spending index decreased by almost 40 percent, falling from 4.14 to 2.79 when the respondent social characteristics are included in the analysis. The effect of that scale is no longer significant.

Table 5.11
Generosity Regressed on
Social Situation and Political Ideology Scales

Respondent Characteristics	B
Gender of respondent (males omitted)	
Female respondents	.19
Race of Respondent (whites omitted)	
Non-white respondents	17.43****
Age of respondent (in yrs)	.25*
Number of Children (older children omitted)	
No children	10.06**
Young babies present	13.84****
Years of school completed	2.30***
Marital Status (married omitted)	
Never married	13.98***
Separated	20.86***
Divorced	5.12
Widowed respondent	-19.89****
Respondent Has Received Welfare	1.41
Employment Status (full time omitted)	
Works part time	3.35
Not working	.42
Retired	35.70****
keeps house	5.32
At school	.68
Respondent Income (divided by 1000)	.015#
Perceived minimum income needed/week	.09****

TABLE 5.11 (cont'd)

	B
Size of City of Residence (rural ommitted)	
Top 12 SMSA's	2.69
Top 100 SMSA's	1.16
Suburb in top 12 SMSA's	7.32
Suburb in top 100 SMSA's	2.97
Counties with 10g+ city	6.50#
Region of residence (New England omitted)	
East south central	-1.44
East north central	1.09
Mid atlantic	-3.73
South atlantic	-5.95
West south central	-13.90*
West north central	15.30***
Mountain region	-13.56*
Pacific region	-17.76***
Political Ideology Scales	
Welfare Beneficial (high=beneficial)	4.19***
Political Ideology (high-con/Rep)	-.03
Roots of Inequality (high=blacks fault)	-1.32
Spending Priorities (high=too much)	-2.79
Government Responsibility (high=no gov)	-2.37***
Constant	149.42****

R Square (respondent level)	.152
Adjusted R Square (respondent level)	.121
R Square (Vignette Level)	.233
Adjusted R Square (vignette level)	.225

N =   970 (6723 vignette ratings)

#	= p < .10
*	= p < .05
**	= p < .01
***	= p < .001
****	= p < .0001

Overall, inclusion of both respondent social standing characteristics and the political scale items produces an R^2 of .152, explaining almost twice the variance in average weekly income award than that explained when only including the political items.

Finally, we examined the overall effect of social standing and political ideology on generosity, in conjunction with the effects found when examining vignette family characteristics. Since the vignette dimensions and respondent characteristics are orthogonal, we should expect no changes in the relative magnitude of the regression coefficients.[10] However, when all respondent characteristics, as well as vignette dimensions and levels are presented, the overall R^2 produced is .233. That is, when taking into account respondent social standing, political persuasion, and the effect of the vignette dimensions and levels, approximately one-fourth of the variance in generosity can be explained.

CONCLUSION

In this chapter, we have examined the extent to which political ideology, as defined by party identification, political practice, and responses to a variety of attitudinal items affects the level of generosity displayed toward welfare families. In all, several salient findings bear repeating here.

1) First, as was predicted, Independents, Democrats, and independents who leaned toward the Democratic Party showed much higher levels of generosity toward the vignette families than Republicans, other independents and third party affiliates. Similarly, the stronger respondents identified with the liberal label, the more generous, with conservatives being less so.

2) Despite these differences when other ideological and social factors were controlled for, party preference and liberal-conservative ideology proved to have virtually no effect on overall levels of generosity.

3) The strongest political ideology predictors of increased generosity are the respondents' perceptions of welfare in general, the extent to which the government has responsibility for addressing inequality and whether the respondent believes more should be spent on human services programs. Respondents who believe government assistance is beneficial to those who are on welfare show much higher levels of generosity. Similarly, respondents who believe the government should stay out of the way with regard to social problems are much less generous than respondents who believe that the government has such a responsibility.

NOTES

1. Note that the proportion of GSS respondents indicating that they voted in 1984 (69.9 percent) is much larger than the proportion of the general, non-institutionalized population that actually voted (approximately 51 percent). The percentage of respondents indicating that they voted for Reagan is only slightly higher than the results for the general population, 60.0 percent and 59 percent respectively.

2. Complete wording of introduction and items can be found in the General Social Survey Codebook. Wording condensed here for space considerations. Responses for "About Right Amount" ommitted from table.

3. Early reports on the 1986 GSS data (c.f Ponza 1988), while acknowledging the disparate responses to the wording of the question, pass over any exploration of the roots of these differences and opt to deal only with the "welfare" version. While agreeing with Ponza et al that excessive effort should not be used to "tease out the 'true' opinions...using these problematic questions dealing with aggregate expenditures," we find it important to acknowledge the differences between the wording of these "problematic" wordings more analytically. The primary purpose of using the factorial survey is to understand these complex differentiations - "Does one respond to a stimulus differently when presented with a second (group) additional stimuli?" - and the method requires that, when found, we expose these differentiations.

4. According to the description and discussion of these items in the GSS codebook, respondents were not to be probed for further response if their initial reaction was to answer "I don't know." However, examination of the marginals for these items indicates that only a small number of persons (approximately 6 percent for the health care item and less than 3 percent for the others) answered "don't know." With these small numbers, and the inability to distinguish the reason for stating such or to what "don't know" refers, these cases are omitted from this analysis.

5.The introduction to this item states "Some people think that the government in Washington ought to reduce income differences between the rich and poor, perhaps by raising the taxes of wealthy families and giving income assistance to the poor. Others think that the government should not concern itself with reducing this income difference..." Respondents were then given a card with a scale ranging from 1 to 7, with one indicating that "The government should do something to reduce income differences between rich and poor", and 7 stating " The government should not concern itself with income differences." Respondents were asked to indicate which "comes closest to the way you feel?"

6. Respondents were given a 5 point scale on which to respond, ranging from "Government Should Help" to Help Selves." For blacks, the last response was "no special treatment." Responses recoded so that 1 and 2 = "Government is obligated" and 4 and 5 = "no special treatment."

7. Note that, for each of these items, the effects of "Welfare" were discussed. As was discussed earlier, there is evidence in the vast differences in responses to items which addressed spending on "welfare," and, more generally, "assistance to the poor." When asked about spending on "welfare," respondents were felt too much had been spent, while too little had been spent on "assistance to poor." Unfortunately, a similar comparison is not possible here because all respondents were given the "welfare" version. We can only speculate if the findings discussed here would have been different had alternative wording been used.

8. This item was actually asked last in this battery of items. It is discussed at this time for comparative purposes.

9. Although this could be addressed by running two separate models in the analysis, for purposes of this analysis a single measure was designed to "tap" respondents concerns with too much government spending. Separate analysis indicated that, although the wording for some of the items elicited different marginal distributions, the effect of the different versions on overall levels of generosity were not significant.

10. For this reason it is not necessary to present those coefficients at this time. See Tables 4.4, and 5.11 for the relative magnitudes of these coefficients.

CHAPTER 6
PUBLIC PERCEPTIONS AND POLITICAL WILL: IMPLICATIONS OF GENEROSITY IN TIMES OF ECONOMIC CONCERN

INTRODUCTION.

Understanding more about the public's perceptions of the needs of the poor can be an effective tool for devising politically acceptable plans for assistance to those less fortunate. For the creation of any substantial public program to assist the poor requires both public support (for those whose re-election depends on such support) and a tax base to provide money to support the program. Public support without the base is good only for display purposes: Raising revenues through taxes without the needed support can be political suicide. Smart legislators--regardless of political persuasion--weigh both aspects (and others) before locking themselves into a position.

What has been presented in the preceding chapters can in many ways be considered an alternative understanding of the public's perceptions of the poor and their willingness to support public assistance programs. And, in many ways, what has been presented can be considered as a liberating tool for those legislators whose support for various legislative initiatives aimed at increasing public assistance wavers with each public opinion poll released.

REVIEW OF MAJOR FINDINGS

Throughout the discussion of the findings, the income awards given to the vignette families were discussed as levels of "generosity." Note, however, that by design the vignette awards more closely represented government provided Aid to Families with Dependent Children awards (AFDC) than any other assistance (e.g. General

Relief). Thus some of the findings, such as the increased awards given for each additional child in the family, were expected.

Note also, however, that respondents were informed prior to being presented with the vignettes that any increases in the weekly income given to these families could result in their paying higher taxes.

Overall Trends

Throughout the analysis presented in the last chapters, two prominent findings appeared time and again. For the most part, these findings seemed to overshadow all other analysis. The most prominent finding presented in this dissertation is the discovery of a monetary barrier, or "floor", below which a vast majority of the American public believes no one should be allowed to fall. Throughout the analysis, the presence of this floor left much of the discussion of variations in generosity without bite. More than 80 percent of the respondents averaged awarding $200 or more per week to the vignette families, regardless of the circumstances presented in the scenario. Less than two percent of the respondents averaged less than $150 per week in award.

The second prominent finding, is that this floor represents over TWICE the average payments that are actually provided by the Government to those persons who are deemed eligible for assistance. Indeed, for a majority of the regions in this country, the average income awarded to the vignette families was more than three times the AFDC awards given to recipients in the lowest supported state for that region (see Figure 4.11).

The overall finding can be summed up as follows: From what can be found in the analysis of the Vignette Supplement to the 1986 General Social Survey, the American public perceives that poor families with children, in almost all circumstances, are deserving of support and that the level of support needed, and approved, is twice the amount currently provided by government programs.

Variations In Generosity: The Driving Forces.

The extent of the analysis presented in the previous chapters is not, of course, limited to the discussion of the existence of this generosity floor. As we examined in Chapters 4 and 5, significant variation in the levels of generosity are found when we examine subgroups of the respondent populations. However, as we also saw in those chapters, not all of the variations were what we expected to find at the outset. In addition, the factorial design utilized in the study was specifically used to examine the variations in generosity shown for families experiencing somewhat different circumstances. The factorial design allows us to examine the underlying influences in respondent generosity, and to uncover the extent to which there is some degree of normative consensus as to what makes one (or one's family) deserving of increased public support.

The examination of the various sub-groups of the respondent population was organized around two basic themes. First, in Chapter 4, differences in generosity were examined in light of respondent demographic and personal characteristics in order to assess the extent to which there was an underlying sympathy or empathy factor that influenced how the vignette families were perceived. That is, do some respondents, because of some similarity in background or experience, "feel" more for the vignette families and thus show more sympathy/empathy for them?

In Chapter 5, we then examined the extent to which the political leanings of the respondent effected the level of generosity exhibited toward the vignette family. In particular, generosity toward the vignette characters was examined in light of the political affiliation of the respondent, and the respondents' perceptions of the role of government and government assistance.

The Vignette Effects: Components of Consensus.

As explained in Chapter 3, the factorial survey design implemented in the GSS study included a number of dimensions on which the stories were built. Computer generation of the vignette scenarios allows us to track which level of the dimensions was included, and to independently analyze how that characteristic affects respondent generosity.

Overall, three vignette characteristics appeared to elicit the highest levels of generosity. For these characteristics, the respondents appeared to be addressing issues facing the family that could be considered beyond the vignette characters' control. First, the number of children present in the family (which is somewhat beyond the immediate control of the vignette character) strongly influenced generosity levels. For those families with more than one child, the weekly income awards given by respondents increased by more than $12 per child, accumulating to almost $50 per week increase for those families with four children.

In addition to the number of children, respondents also showed increased levels of generosity for vignette characters who were unemployed, but actively looking for gainful employment. If the mother worked part time, or could not work because of child care needs, respondents also awarded higher weekly income awards, although those increases were not statistically significant.

Note, however, that in the vignette scenarios where the characters were not actively looking for such employment, respondents displayed punitive reactions, decreasing the weekly awards substantially. This is particularly evident for those scenarios where the vignette family mother was picky about where to work (e.g. jobs that only paid minimum wage), in which respondents decreased the weekly award by more than $20.

The vignette scenarios that elicited the largest increases in generosity, however, were those in which the father of the children was disabled. For those families, respondents increase the weekly award more than $25 over similar families where the father was employed.

Thus, it appears that the vignette characteristics which elicited the highest levels of generosity are those in which the problems facing the family appear to be beyond the immediate control of the individual family depicted--large family composition, unemployment, and physical disabilities. In addition, respondents respond much more positively to those who, despite the hardship, are still actively working to help themselves get out their difficulties. As long as the vignette families are trying to help themselves, respondents appear much more sympathetic and are much more willing to help out as well.

Generosity: Vulnerability and Sympathy.

In addition to increased levels of generosity being found for those scenarios with vignette characteristics which elicit sympathy, in Chapter 4 we found that sympathy/empathy factors are also important when examining respondent characteristics. That is, respondents who are in similar situations, and who are in subgroups of the population would appear to be in similarly vulnerable situations, also show higher levels of support for the vignette families than those who are better off.

Overall, generosity levels were influenced significantly by several respondent demographic characteristics, including the race of the respondent, marital status, family composition and education. Non-white respondents showed much higher levels of generosity than whites, awarding almost $20 per week more in weekly income than whites when all other characteristics are controlled for. This finding was particularly striking for non-white female respondents.

Single and previously married (divorced and separated) respondents also showed increased levels of generosity, averaging an award of more than $15 per week in income awards than married respondents, and almost $40 per week more than widows and widowers. In addition, those respondents with young babies in their household showed higher levels of generosity than those whose children are older, with an average increase in income award of more than $16 per week.

Finally, respondents who most benefit from government assistance, particularly those who have received public assistance and retired persons on fixed incomes (either in part or completely received from Social Security) show very high levels of generosity when compared to their younger, working counterparts. Indeed, retired persons average more than $35 more per week in income awards than those persons who are currently employed full time--the single strongest impact seen from any of the respondent characteristics when all other factors are controlled.

Political Persuasion and Generosity.

Perhaps the most significant finding from Chapter 5 and the examination of the political and ideological scales employed is the lack of any influence on generosity toward the poor found when examining the political affiliation characteristics. As we saw in Chapter 5, when we control for other respondent characteristics we find virtually no variations in generosity when comparing political party affiliation and along the liberal-conservative self identification measures. Although some differences can be seen when we examine the overall differences in levels of generosity between Republicans and Democrats, when other factors, particularly respondent demographic characteristics, these differences diminish.

The two ideological positions that affect generosity levels, however, concern less tangible political positions. Again, what appears to drive a good deal of generosity toward the vignette families is less a political position an more of a "golden rule" perspective. The more strongly respondents see the government as responsible for the alleviation of hardship caused by poverty, the higher the generosity shown toward families in need. Similarly, the more successful and beneficial one perceives public assistance programs, the stronger the support for those families who partake in those programs.

Thus the primary ideological influences appear to be symptoms of government (and poverty program advocate) marketing problems-- if public assistance programs are seen as important, and if they are seen as beneficial, public support for their implementation grows. Skepticism about the merits of such programs decreases their public support base.

LIMITATIONS, IMPLICATIONS, AND SPECULATIONS

The statement above that differences in generosity appear to be linked to marketing problems associated with design and implementation of public assistance programs is meant as a tongue in cheek indictment of program opponents and advocates alike. The image of selling programs to the public (or, for that matter, elected officials), while in some ways are accurate, implies a cynical view of the American public and how public opinion is formed. We would hope Americans are discriminating in forming opinions, and cannot be easily sold the proverbial bill of goods.

Such marketing techniques are often employed to both to sell and to fight public assistance programs. Ronald Reagan, in his 1980 campaign for president, frequently cited abuses within the welfare system as proof that such abuse is the norm, and that the American public shouldn't support such freeloaders. Welfare has, as a result, taken on a primarily negative association, with apparently low levels of public support (Smith, 1987). Similarly, campaigns by advocates calling for increased assistance program funding are quick to use television and print media pieces to show the prevalence of infants and children in the poverty ranks as proof of the inadequacy of the programs. From what we have seen in this dissertation, the assistance advocates are by far closer to the public nerve than the opponents.

The results of this study show that, contrary to the anti-welfare rhetoric used in political campaigns, the American public strongly supports public assistance when faced with real (or in this case modeled to represent real) circumstances depicting those in need. To be sure, the vast majority of the American public discriminates between circumstances in awarding such assistance. Such support is still prevalent, however, even for those who the political speech writers would tell us are abusing the assistance programs by not working or looking for work.

This is not to say that the previous analysis presented here is the definitive statement on public support of public assistance programs. From this analysis it is clear that the commonly assumed (by pundits and politicians) public opposition to welfare programs for the poor has little support when public opinion is more systematically examined.

The results from this study also give support to welfare reform advocates who seek to improve the coverage and the extent of public assistance in order to insure that no one in this country slips through a safety net offered by social welfare programs offering economic assistance. Properly channeled, the extent of this support could lead to drastic improvements in coverage of these programs, and to the realignment of the political and economic agenda of this nation.

Limitations of the Study.

As with all studies, limitations in this study require us to use some caution before making too grandiose claims about the results presented. And, as with all studies, there are aspects of the project that would be conducted differently were we to replicate this effort. Overall, the two primary areas in which such limitations are at issue here concern somewhat general limitations of the factorial survey technique employed and more specific limitations in the final design of the vignette dimensions and levels.

Vignette Composition Limitations.

The primary limitations within the vignette composition and design are the omission of several important dimensions and levels, and the extent to which the rating scale adequately measured the perceptions of the poor family depicted in the scenario. Although time constraints were a major factor in the deign of these vignettes, minor changes could be implemented in the vignette composition and response scales used which could greatly improve the analysis. As can be recalled from Chapter 4, several of these dimensions, when examined within the respondent characteristics, would appear to have some important effect on the levels of generosity.

Two forms of omissions are, we believe, important for discussion here. The most straightforward omission from the vignette design is the absence of variation in the race of the vignette family. Non-white respondents showed much higher levels of generosity toward the vignette families than did whites, strongly supporting, as was suggested in chapter 4, that sympathy/empathy toward these families was in large part based on similarity between respondents experiences and those of the vignette families. In addition, popular presentation of poor families in such media as television often portray blacks in lower socio-economic roles. It can only be speculated, because of the omission of a race dimension in the vignette design, that such presentation would lead to stereotyping of welfare recipients as primarily minorities, and lower overall generosity.

A second important omission in the vignette design was that of the role of the male in the household. By design, there were no male-headed households without a female present. Little was known about the male's education, or circumstances why the male was not looking for a job (if not in prison). Information on the type, and extent, of disability was also not included--ruling out potentially important comparisons of, for example, whether a mental handicap or impairment was perceived as more deserving of assistance than physical disability or problems associated with substance abuse. Similarly, there was no attempt in the design to assess the extent to which poor, single, childless adults (male or female) deserve assistance. Ideally, inclusion of single non-parents would serve as an important baseline for comparison.

In addition to changes in the composition of the vignette scenario, future efforts examining perceptions of the poor should also include variations in the design, and possibly number of, rating scales used in the analysis. In the study presented here, a single rating scale was used, asking respondents to mark on the scale (ranging from $0 to $600) the weekly income award the family depicted in the vignette should receive. In addition, the instructions indicated that any increase in income could "affect the taxes you (the respondent) pays," and that responses were to include both money already received, and any government assistance the family may need.

In retrospect, however, several omissions seem to have been made when designing the rating scale that could have greatly improved the analysis. First, no information was obtained (either in the vignette component or the primary survey instrument) as to the extent of respondent knowledge concerning how much government assistance families such as those depicted in the vignettes were eligible for according to government regulations. What do respondents know about AFDC, General Assistance, and other government welfare programs? Obtaining such information, particularly in light of the discussion in Chapter 1 (and Chapter 4) of the vast differences in eligibility requirements and benefit levels awarded by different states, would prove particularly useful in understanding respondent generosity level differences. Remember from Chapter 4 that despite vast differences in the real benefit levels awarded, only marginal differences were found in respondent generosity between regions.

In addition to gaining information about respondent understanding of actual assistance programs and awards, future efforts should also include a separate rating item looking at the bottom line. That is, in addition to (or instead of) asking respondents to rate how much money the vignette families should receive, items that address how much respondents are willing to pay in additional taxes if that tax money were to go to assist families such as those depicted should be included. Similarly, items that address where additional revenues could come from (for example cuts in defense spending, foreign aid, or perhaps farm subsidies to pay for additional public assistance payments), would be useful for more systematic assessment of the policy implications of our findings.

General Limitations.

In addition to the more specific limitations in vignette design mentioned above, a set of more general limitations and shortcomings with the 1986 GSS study are also cause for caution. First, because of the limited number of vignettes presented to each respondent (seven depicting young families) some caution is necessary in assessing the impact of the various dimensions and levels. Although by design there is no systematic bias in the allocation of vignettes to individuals, by limiting the number of scenarios per packet to seven, we are less assured that individuals received a representative allotment. This is not to say that the analysis is necessarily flawed, but rather indicates respondents may not have received as broad a range of interaction between various dimensions and levels with this number of vignettes (for example, the different marital status levels with each of the employment levels) as they would have with more. If respondents had received more vignettes, say 30 per person, more systematic analysis of variations within individual respondents could have been attempted.

Second, and to some critics of the factorial survey method the most problematic limitation, is what could be called the "problem of the hypothetical." That is, the analysis here and the discussion of generosity among respondents centers on responses to hypothetical families who are at or near the poverty line. These families are not real in the sense that the respondent knows them, and therefore, some critics argue any generosity shown toward the vignette characters is done so without any real costs to the respondent. The respondents are not actually forced to pay out of pocket cash to cover the increased income awarded. The statement prior to the completion of the packet only suggests that in the long run taxes may be levied. Thus responses indicating high levels of generosity are easily dismissed by critics as socially correct responses that do not easily lend themselves to interpretation.

Although there is some basis to the claim that there is no direct cost to the respondents, and thus it is easier to be generous, the results bear out that respondents discriminate between the various factors in the scenarios. As we saw above, respondents read the vignettes with a critical eye. Much more generosity was found for those vignettes where the families condition was beyond their control (disabled, or involuntarily unemployed), than for those who could be considered more culpable for their situation. Even if these levels of generosity were somewhat elevated because of the "hypothetical" nature of the scenarios, an understanding of the normative structure of that generosity is possible.

Even more important, however, remember that the hypothetical nature of these or any stories is not only an issue with regard to this study. In deliberations carried out in the legislatures, all laws are concerned with hypothetical situations. Discussions over funding for a new fighter bomber for the military center on a hypothetical craft which, given funding, someone would like to build. Similarly, discussions of welfare reform focus on how proposed welfare programs will help hypothetical or stereotypical welfare families. Seldom do we see actual poor people brought before legislative bodies for their testimony (although the use of actual homeless people may have had a positive effect on deliberations of the Mc-Kinney Act).

POLICY IMPLICATIONS AND RECOMMENDATIONS: WHAT CAN BE DONE?

The concern of the hypothetical nature of the factorial survey vignettes is most important with regard to development of public policy. When discussing the implications of these results we must keep in mind that the generosity levels discussed here are **opinions and perceptions** of what these families deserve. From the structure uncovered here, more informed policy discussion and planning can be carried out which utilizes these insights. With this in mind, therefore, three primary implications and recommendations for policy development can be made.

Payment Levels.

The high level of generosity exhibited by a vast majority of the respondents to the vignette scenarios has been a main point of focus throughout the analysis and discussion of the results from the GSS study. The actual payments made to families on AFDC and other such programs are drastically lower than the income levels awarded to these vignette families. Even if, as some critics would argue, these levels are somewhat inflated because of the fictitious nature of the vignettes, the implications of high levels of generosity are still strong.

The American public believes public assistance recipients deserve a lot more money than the government awards. Decrease the amount of award by 50 percent to adjust for the extra generosity critics attribute to the hypothetical nature of the design, and we would still find vast differences between what is actually paid to welfare recipients, and what the public feels is needed. And, as seems clear from this study, the American public is not naive about where the money would come from to pay for these program expenditure increases. Everyone knows that the revenue would have to come from taxes, yet it seems clear that our respondents support such revenue allocation for those families in need.

Assistance levels, in constant dollars, have decreased precipitously over the past two decades. It can easily be concluded from this study that the public has recognized such declines, even if the legislature has not. We strongly recommended, therefore, that the levels of funding be increased to at least match the inflationary change, and preferably for those increases to be enough to offer those in need a decent life.

Specific Program Support.

In the standard survey items, majorities of the respondents supported increased funding for a variety of human needs programs. In the vignette component of the study, support for current programs becomes even more evident.

Two primary welfare programs are addressed in the GSS vignettes. Most obvious is the association of the vignette families with Aid to Families with Dependent Children program (AFDC). All of the vignette scenarios involved families with young children. And, as we saw, generosity levels increased for increased numbers of children. Note also, however, that this is a benefit to the most vulnerable segment of the population--young children. It is not argued here that the increased support is aimed at the adults in the family. The circumstances of the adult have differing effects on generosity, depending in the extent to which the adults are "trying to help themselves."

In short, support for the AFDC program in particular appears to be very strong, and the importance of that program obvious. In addition to assistance programs for families with young children, the respondents also appear to support those welfare programs that assist the disabled. In particular, in those instances where the father of the children depicted in the vignette scenario was disabled[1], the level of generosity increased significantly, with increases averaging more than $26 per week (p < .0000, see Table 4.3). Thus, again, we find that the public is strongly supportive of, in particular, those programs that are designed to assist the portion of the American population which, like the disabled and young children, cannot easily take care of itself. It is thus imperative that such programs be maintained.

The National Case.

Finally, there is strong evidence to suggests that the welfare reform should focus on the creation of national standards for setting eligibility requirements and benefit levels. A strong case has been made by prominent researchers for the creation of such national standards (c.f. Rossi, 1989; Shapiro and Greenstein, 1988). The creation of uniform requirements and benefit levels would allow for more of those persons who need assistance to be able to obtain help, and for fewer children and disabled persons to be destitute.

Despite the drastic differences in assistance levels that actually exists between regions of the countries and from state to state, support for a high level of support remains constant throughout the country. In all sections of the country we find the vast majority of the American public supports a standard of living for the poor that ranges from two to five times higher than the government offers. For program advocates, a national campaign for standardization of requirements and benefit levels would appear to be in the cards if this support can be mobilized.

CONCLUSION

Addressing the implications and implement the recommendations discussed above will not come cheaply. Little in the realm of public assistance ever comes cheaply. These improvements can, however, come at a bargain. At the time of this writing several drastically different, yet equally important changes are taking place that demand these changes be examined. On the home front, the "War On Poverty" has been replaced by the "War on Drugs," which rages on without a true battle field. Poverty, particularly urban poverty and homelessness, at times seems to be omnipresent. Talk of welfare reform on Capitol Hill often does little to address these problems, much less the roots from which they grow. If the problems of drugs, poverty and homelessness are to be addressed, government priorities on both the local and national level must be re-examined and changed.

Proposals for increased assistance levels and coverage will cost millions of dollars. To ignore the need for these increases will, however, cost much more in the long run. The decline in quality educational attainment by our children is a direct result of the deterioration in health, education, and welfare programs. At the same time of these declines, military might and adventurism seem to have regained prestige. Federal expenditures for Aid to Families with Dependent Children (AFDC) increased almost $4 billion 1980 and 1986--about the same as the reported cost of the Stealth Bomber program.

On the international front, over the past several years, and particularly since 1989, we have seen dramatic changes in international relations. First, military concern over the Communist Block countries can be reexamined now that many of these countries have thrown out the "Old Guard" as personified by the Central Communist Party. Democracy may well flourish in the East--a boon to peace while a disaster for the Military Industrial complex.

At the same time, however, the economic re-organization of Western Europe is cause for alarm for the United States economic analysts. A strong European Economic Community (EEC) will pose new problems for American corporations in their attempt to compete abroad with the Japanese. Fears of being second in the trade war with Japan could be replaced by being relegated to the Bronze medal slot in the economic Olympics.

With the mix of our national problems and international re-organization the United States is at a crossroads where decisions must be made quickly. Like the business proverb states, we must tighten our belt and deal with the problems facing us. Unlike the proverb, however, we cannot afford to sink into the mentality that "someone has to suffer" and that we have to "suck it up," for the suffering that would occur threatens to destroy the very underpinnings of this country many believe have made us fairly successful.

It seems apparent from the study presented here that the American public believes emphasis must be placed on insuring individuals in this country are protected from the misery of poverty. In order to carry this out, the government must place the economic priorities of this country on insuring this protection. Military might is no match for the social and economic changes taking place abroad. And, indeed, military might has failed to deal with the drug and crime problems at home.

NOTES

1. As can be recalled from earlier discussions, the only dimension that included a level for disabilities was for the father of the children depicted. No mention was made for disabilities for the mother.

REFERENCES

Anderson, A.B., A. Harris, and J. Miller. 1983. "Models of Deterrence Theory." *Social Science Research, 12:236-262.*

Bonnet-Brunnich, Patricia. 1984. *Perceptions of Fairness in Social Security Retirement Benefits.* Unpublished Dissertation, University of Wisconsin, Madison.

Cook, Fay Lomax. 1979. *Who Should Be Helped: Public Support for Social Services.* Beverly Hills: Sage Publications.

Cook, Fay Lomax, E.J. Barrett, S. J. Popkin, E.A. Constantino, and J. E. Kaufman. 1988. *Convergent Perspectives on Social Welfare Policy: The Views From the General Public, Members of Congress, and AFDC Recipients.* Center For Urban Affairs and Policy Research, Evanston, Il. Executive Report to the Ford Foundation.

Davis, James Allan and Tom W. Smith 1986. *The General Social Surveys 1972-1986.* [machine readable data file] Principle Investigator James A. Davis; Senior Study Director, Tom W. Smith. NORC ed. Chicago: National Opinion Research Center, producer, 1986; Storrs, CT: The Roper Center for Public Opinion Research, University of Connecticut, distributor. Data file (20,056 logical records) and codebook.

Hasenfeld Yeheskel, and Jane A. Rafferty 1989. "The Determinants of Public Attitudes Toward the Welfare State." *Social Forces, 67:4.*

Kluegel, James R. and Elliot R. Smith 1986. *Beliefs About Inequality: American's Views of What Ought to Be.* New York: Aldine DeGruyter.

Love, Lois Thessien. 1986. *The Extent of Public Obligation: Minimally Acceptable Living Conditions as Perceived by Chicago Area Voters.* Unpublished dissertation, University of Chicago.

Pereira, Joseph 1986. *Who Should Be Supported: New Yorkers Normative Views of Welfare Entitlement.* Unpublished Dissertation, University of Massachusetts, Amherst.

Ponza, Michael, Greg J. Duncan, Mary Corcoran and Fred Groskind 1988. "The Guns of Autumn? Age Differences in Support for Income Transfers To the Young and Old." Unpublished research paper, Survey Research Center, University of Michigan.

Rossi, Peter H. 1989. *Down and Out In America: The Origins of Homelessness.* Chicago: University of Chicago Press.

Rossi, P.H and A. B. Anderson 1982 "The Factorial Survey Approach: An Introduction." in P. H. Rossi and S. L. Nock (eds) *Measuring Social Judgements: The Factorial Survey Approach, Beverly Hills, Sage.*

Rossi, Peter H. and Richard A. Berk, 1985. "Varieties of Normative Consensus," *American Sociological Review, vol 50:333-347.*

Rossi, Peter H. and Steven L. Nock, eds., 1982. *Measuring Social Judgments: The Factorial Survey Approach, Sage publications.*

Rossi, P. H. and E. Weber-Burdin 1983 "Sexual Harassment on the Campus" Amherst, MA, Social and Demographic Research Institute, University of Massachusetts, Amherst.

Rossi, P. H. and Jeffry A. Will 1985 "The Dimensions of Interpersonal Ties: A Factorial Survey Approach," Social and Demographic Research Institute University of Massachusetts, Amherst.

St. John, Craig and Nancy A. Bates 1990 "Racial Composition and Neighborhood Evaluation." *Social Science Research.* 19,1: 47-61.

Schiltz, Michael E. 1970. *Public Attitudes Toward Social Security, 1935-1965.* Washington D.C., U.S. Government Printing Office.

Shapiro, Issaac, and R. Greenstein. 1988. *Holes in the Safety Net: Poverty Programs and Policies in the States.* Washington D.C., Center On Budget and Policy Priorities.

Shapiro, Robert Y. and K.D. Patterson, J. Russell and J. T. Young. 1987 (a) "The Polls: Public Assistance." *Public Opinion Quarterly.* 51:120-130.

_____ 1987 (b) "The Polls: Employment and Public Welfare." *Public Opinion Quarterly.* 51:268-281.

Shapiro, Robert Y. and J. T. Young 1986 "The Polls: Medical Care in the United States." *Public Opinion Quarterly.* 50:418-428.

_____. 1989. "Public Opinion and the Welfare State: The United States In Comparative Perspective." *Political Science Quarterly.* 104,1:59-89.

Sidel, Ruth 1987. *Women and Children Last: The Plight of Poor Women In Affluent America.* Penguin Books, New York.

Smith, Tom W. 1987. "That Which We Call By Any Other Name Would Smell Sweeter: An Analysis of the Impact of Question Wording On Response Patterns." *Public Opinion Quarterly.* 51,1:75 - 83.

Sitaraman, Bhavani 1990. *Public Attitudes Toward Abortion.* Unpublished Dissertation, University of Massachusetts, Amherst.

Thurman, Q., J. Lam, and P. H. Rossi. 1988. "Sorting Out the Cookoo's Nest" *Sociological Quarterly, 29,4:565-588.*

United States Department of Commerce 1989. *The Statistical Abstracts of the United States, Washington D.C.:* U.S. Government Printing Office.